Astounding Stories of S

November, 1

Various

Alpha Editions

This edition published in 2024

ISBN : 9789367247990

Design and Setting By
Alpha Editions
www.alphaedis.com
Email - info@alphaedis.com

And then Kay had broken through and was hewing madly with great sweeps of the ax.

The Wall of Death

By Victor Rousseau

This news," said Cliff Hynes, pointing to the newspaper, "means the end of *homo Americanus*."

> Out of the Antarctic it came—a wall of viscid, grey, half-human jelly, absorbing and destroying all life that it encountered.

The newspaper in question was the hour-sheet of the International Broadcast Association, just delivered by pneumatic tube at the laboratory. It was stamped 1961, Month 13, Day 7, Horometer 3, and the headlines on the front page confirmed the news of the decisive defeat of the American military and naval forces at the hands of the Chinese Republic.

A gallant fight for days against hopeless odds; failure of the army dynamos; airships cut off from ground guidance; battleships ripped to pieces by the Chinese disintegrators; and, finally, the great wave of black death that had wiped out two hundred thousand men.

Kay Bevan—to use the old-fashioned names which still persisted, despite the official numerical nomenclature—glanced through the account. He threw the sheet away. "We deserved it, Cliff," he said.

Cliff nodded. "You saw that bit about the new Chinese disintegrator? If the Government had seriously considered our Crumbler—"

Kay glanced at the huge, humming top that filled the center of the laboratory. It spun so fast that it appeared as nothing but a spherical shadow, through which one could see the sparse furnishings, the table, the apparatus ranged upon it, and the window over-looking the upper streets of New York.

"Yes—*if!*" he answered bitterly. "And I'm willing to bet the Chinese have an inferior machine, built upon the plans that Chinese servant stole from us last year."

"We deserved it, Cliff," said Kay again. "For ten years we've harried and enslaved the yellow man, and taken a hundred thousand of his men and women to sacrifice to the Earth Giants. What would we have done, if conditions had been reversed?"

"Self-preservation," Cliff suggested.

"Exactly. The law of the survival of the fittest. They thought that they were fitter to survive. I tell you they had right on their side, Cliff, and that's what's beaten us. Now—a hundred thousand of our *own* boys and girls must be fed into the maw of these monsters every year. God, suppose it were Ruth!"

"Or you or I," said Cliff. "If only we could perfect the Crumbler!"

"What use would that be against the Earth Giants? There's nothing organic about them, not even bones. Pure protoplasm!"

"We could have used it against the Chinese," said Cliff. "Now—" He shrugged his shoulders hopelessly.

And if explorers had been content to leave the vast unknown Antarctic Continent alone, they would never have taught the imprisoned Giants to cross the great ice barrier. But that crossing had taken place fifteen years ago, and already the mind of man had become accustomed to the grim facts.

Who could have dreamed that the supposed table-land was merely a rim of ice-mountains, surrounding a valley twice the size of Europe, so far below sea-level that it was warmed to tropic heat by Earth's interior fires? Or that this valley was peopled with what could best be described as organized protoplasm?

Enormous, half-transparent, gelatinous organism, attaining a height of about a hundred feet, and crudely organized into forms not unlike those of men?

Half the members of the Rawlins Expedition, which had first entered this valley, had fallen victims to the monsters. Most of the rest had gone raving mad. And the stories of the two who returned, sane, to Buenos Aires, were discredited and scoffed at as those of madmen.

But of a second expedition none had survived, and it was the solitary survivor of the third who had confirmed the amazing story. The giant monsters, actuated by some flickering human intelligence, had found their way out of the central valley, where they had subsisted by enfolding their vegetable and small animal prey with pseudopods, that it to say, temporary projections of arms from the gelatinous bulk of their substance.

They had floated across the shallow seas between the tip of the Antarctic Continent and Cape Horn, as toy balloons float on water. Then they had spread northward, extending in a wall that reached from the Atlantic to the Andes. And, as they moved, they had devoured all vegetables and animal life in their path. Behind them lay one great bare, absolutely lifeless area.

How many of them were there? That was the hideous fact that had to be faced. Their numbers could not be counted because, after attaining a height of about a hundred feet, they reproduced by budding!

And within a few weeks these buds, in turn, attained their full development.

The Argentine Government had sent a force of twenty thousand men against them, armed with cannon, machine-guns, tanks, airplanes, poison gas, and the new death-ray. And in the night, when it was bivouacking, after what it had thought was glorious victory, it had been overwhelmed *and eaten*!

Proof against the poison gas, the hideous monsters were, and invulnerable to shot and shell. Divided and sub-divided, slashed into ribbons, blown to fragments by bombs, each of the pieces simply became the nucleus of a new organism, able, within a few hours, to assume the outlines of a dwarf man, and to seize and devour its prey.

But the Argentine expedition had done worse than it at first dreamed of. *It had given the monsters a taste for human flesh!*

After that, the wave of devastation had obliterated life in every city clear up to the Amazonian forests. And then it had been discovered that, by feeding these devils human flesh, they could be rendered torpid and their advance stayed—so long as the periodical meals continued!

At first criminals had been supplied them, then natives, then Chinese, obtained by periodical war raids. What would you have? The savage regions of the earth had already been depopulated, and a frenzy of fear had taken possession of the whole world.

Now the Chinese had defeated the annual American invasion, and the Earth Giants were budding and swarming through the heart of Brazil.

"Man," said the Theosophists, "is the fifth of the great root-races that have inhabited this planet. The fourth were the Atlanteans. The third were the Lemurians, half-human beings of whom the Australian aborigines are the survivors. The second race was not fully organized into human form. Of the first, nothing is known.

"These are the second race, surviving in the Antarctic valleys. Half-human objects, groping toward that perfection of humanity of which we ourselves fall very far short. As the Kabbala says, man, before Adam, reached from heaven to earth."

Kay Bevan and Cliff Hynes had been working feverishly to perfect their Crumbler for use in the Chinese wars. Convinced, as were all fair-minded men, that these annual raids were unjustified, they yielded to the logic of the facts. Should America sacrifice a hundred thousand of her boys and girls each year, when human life was cheap in China? *Boys and girls!*

It had been discovered that the Earth Giants required the flesh of women as well as of men. Some subtle chemical constituent then produced the state of torpidity during which the advance and the budding of the monsters was stayed. During the ten past years their northward advance had been almost inappreciable. Brazil had even sent another army against them.

But the deadliest gases had failed to destroy the tenacious life of these protoplasmic creatures, and the tanks, which had driven through and through them, had become entangled and blocked in the gelatinous exudations, and their occupants eaten.

All over the world scientists were striving to invent some way of removing this menace to the world. Moreover, airplanes sent to the polar continent had reported fresh masses mobilizing for the advance northward. A second wave would probably burst through the Amazon forest barrier and sweep over the Isthmus and overrun North America.

Five days after the news of the Chinese disaster was confirmed, Cliff Hynes came back from the capital of the American Confederation, Washington.

"It's no use, Kay," he said. "The Government won't even look at the Crumbler. I told them it would disintegrate every inorganic substance to powder, and they laughed at me. And it's true, Kay: they've given up the attempt to enslave China. Henceforward a hundred thousand of our own citizens are to be sacrificed each year. Eaten alive, Kay! God, if only the Crumbler would destroy organic forms as well!"

The first year's quota of fifty thousand boys and fifty thousand girls, thrown to the maw of the monsters to save humanity, nearly disrupted the Confederation. Despite the utmost secrecy, despite the penalty of death for publishing news of the sacrifice, despite the fact that those who drew the fatal lots were snatched from their homes at dead of night, everything became known.

On the vast pampas in the extreme north of the Argentine Republic, where Bolivia, the Argentine, Paraguay and Brazil unite, was the place of sacrifice. Thousands of acres, white with the bones of those whom the monsters had engulfed. Brainless, devoid of intelligence, sightless, because even the sense had not become differentiated in them, yet by some infernal instinct the Earth Giants had become aware that this was their feasting ground.

By some tacit compact, the guards who had annually brought their victims to be devoured had been unmolested, the vast wall of semi-human shapes withdrawing into the shelter of the surrounding forests while the Chinese were staked out in rows. Death, which would have been a mercy, had been denied them. It was living flesh that the Earth Giants craved. And here, on the spot known as Golgotha, the hideous sacrifice had been annually repeated.

That first year, when the chosen victims were transported to the fatal spot, all America went mad. Frenzied parents attacked the offices of the Federation in every city. The cry was raised that Spanish Americans had been selected in preference to those of more northern blood. Civil war loomed imminent.

And year after year these scenes must be repeated. Boys and girls, from fifteen to twenty years of age, the flower of the Federation, a hundred thousand of them, must die a hideous death to save humanity. Now the choice of the second year's victims was at hand.

In their laboratory, removed to the heart of the Adirondacks wilderness, Cliff and Kay were working frantically.

"It's the last chance, Kay," said Cliff. "If I've not solved the secret this time, it means another year's delay. The secret of dissolving organic forms as well as inorganic ones! What is this mysterious power that enables organic forms to withstand the terrific bombardment of the W-ray?"

The W-ray was the Millikan cosmic ray, imprisoned and adapted for human use. It was a million times more powerful than the highest known voltage of electricity. Beneath it, even the diamond, the hardest substance known, dissolved into a puff of dust; and yet the most fragile plant growth remained unaffected.

The laboratory in the Adirondacks was open at one end. Here, against a background of big forest trees, a curious medley of substances had been assembled: old chairs, a couple of broken-down airplanes, a large disused dynamo, a heap of discarded clothing, a miscellany of kitchen utensils on a table, a gas stove, and a heap of metal junk of all kinds. The place looked, in fact, like a junk heap.

The great top was set in a socket in a heavy bar of craolite, the new metal that combined the utmost tensile strength with complete infusibility, even in the electric furnace. About six feet in height, it looked like nothing but what it was, a gyroscope in gimbals, with a long and extremely narrow slit extending all around the central bulge, but closed on the operator's side by a sliding cover of the same craolite.

Within this top, which, by its motion, generated a field of electrical force between the arms of an interior magnet, the W-rays were generated in accordance with a secret formula; the speed of gyration, exceeding anything known on earth, multiplied their force a billionfold, converting them to wave-lengths shorter than the shortest known to physical science. Like all great inventions, the top was of the simplest construction.

"Well," said Cliff, "you'd better bring out Susie."

Kay left the laboratory and went to the cabin beside the lake that the two men occupied. From her box in front of the stove a lady porcupine looked up lazily and grunted. Kay raised the porcupine; in the box, of course. Susie was constitutionally indolent, but one does not handle porcupines, however smooth their quills may lie.

Kay brought her to the heap of junk and placed the box on top of it. He went inside the laboratory. "I may as well tell you, Cliff. I wouldn't have brought Susie if I'd thought the experiment had the least chance of success," he said.

Cliff said nothing. He was bending over the wheel, adjusting a micrometer. "All ready, Kay?" he asked.

Kay nodded and stepped back. He swallowed hard. He hated sacrificing Susie to the cause of science; he almost hoped the experiment would fail.

Cliff pressed a lever, and slowly the ponderous top began to revolve upon its axis. Faster, faster, till it was nothing but a blur. Faster yet, until only its outlines were visible. Cliff pressed a lever on the other side.

Nothing happened apparently, except for a cloudy appearance of the air at the open end of the laboratory. Cliff touched a foot lever. The top began to grow visible, its rotations could be seen; it ran slower, began to come to a stop.

The cloud was gone. Where the airplanes and other junk had been, was nothing but a heap of grayish dust. It was this that had made the cloud.

Nothing remained, except that impalpable powder against the background of the trees.

Kay caught Cliff's arm. "Look out!" he shouted, pointing to the heap. "Something's moving in there!"

Something was. A very angry lady porcupine was scrambling out, a *quillless* porcupine, with a white skin, looking like nothing so much as a large, hairless rat. Cliff turned to Kay.

"We've failed," he said briefly. "Too late for this year now."

"But—the quills?"

"Inorganic material. But even the bones remain intact because there's circulation in the marrow, you see. And the Earth Giants haven't even bones. They're safe—this year!"

He flung himself down under a tree, staring up at the sky in abject despair.

"Look, Kay, I've got my number!" Ruth Meade smiled as she handed Kay the ticket issued by the Government announcing the lottery number provided for each citizen.

One hundred thousand young people between the ages of fifteen and twenty would be drawn for the sacrifice, and Ruth, being nineteen, had come within the limits, but this would be her last year. In a few weeks the Government would announce the numbers—drawn by a second lottery—of those who were condemned.

Then, before these had been made public, the victims would already have been seized and hurried to the airship depots in a hundred places, for conveyance to the hideous Golgotha of the pampas.

The chance that any individual would be among the fated ones was reasonably small. It was the fashion to make a jest of the whole business. Ruth smiled as she showed her ticket.

Kay stared at it. "Ruth, if—if anything happened to you I'd go insane. I'd—"

"Why this sudden ardor, Kay?"

Kay took Ruth's small hand in his. "Ruth, you mustn't play with me any more. You know I love you. And the sight of that thing makes me almost insane. You do care, don't you?" And, as Ruth remained silent, "Ruth, it isn't Cliff Hymes, is it? I know you two are old friends. I'd rather it were Cliff than anybody else, if it had to be some one, but—tell me, Ruth!"

"It isn't Cliff," said Ruth slowly.

"Is it—some one else?"

"It's you, dear," answered Ruth. "It's always been you. It might have been Cliff if you hadn't come along. But he knows now it can never be he."

"Does he know it's me?" asked Kay, greatly relieved.

Ruth inclined her head. "He took it very finely," she said. "He said just what you've said about him. Oh, Kay, if only your experiment had succeeded, and the world could be free of this nightmare! What happened? Why couldn't you and Cliff make it destroy life?"

"I don't know, dear," answered Kay. "Iron and steel melt into powder at the least impact of the rays. They are so powerful that there was even a leakage through the rubber and anelektron container. Even the craolite socket was partly fused, and that is supposed to be an impossibility. And there was a hole in the ground seven feet deep where the very mineral water in the earth had been dissolved. But against organic substances the W-ray is powerless.

"Next year, dear—next year we'll have solved our problem, and then we'll free the world of this menace, this nightmare. Ruth—don't let's talk about that now. I love you!"

They kissed. The Earth Giants faded out of their consciousness even while Ruth held that ominous ticket in her hand.

Kay said nothing to Cliff about it, but Cliff knew. Perhaps he had put his fate to the test with Ruth and learned the truth from her. Ruth made no reference to the matter when she saw Kay. But between the two men, friends for years, a coolness was inexorably developing.

They had gone to work on the new machine. They were hopeful. When they were working, they forgot their rivalry.

"You see, Kay," said Cliff, "we mustn't forget that the Millikan rays have been bombarding Earth since Earth became a planet, out of the depths of space. It is their very nature not to injure organic life, otherwise all life on Earth would have been destroyed long ago. Now, our process is only an adaptation of these cosmic rays. We haven't changed their nature."

"No," agreed Kay. "What we want is a death-ray strong enough to obliterate these monsters, without simply disintegrating them and creating new fragments to bud into the complete being. Why do you suppose they are so tenacious of life, Cliff?"

"They represent primeval man, life itself, striving to organize itself, and nothing is more tenacious than the life principle," answered Cliff.

Meanwhile the fatal weeks were passing. A few days after the tickets had been distributed, a Government notice was broadcasted and published, ordaining that, in view of former dissensions, no substitutes for the condemned persons would be permitted. Rich or poor, each of the victims chosen by lot must meet his fate.

And the monsters were growing active. There had been an extension of their activities. Tongues had been creeping up the rivers that ran into the Amazon. Suddenly a dense mass of the devils had appeared on the north coast, near Georgetown. They had overleaped the Amazon; they were overrunning British Guiana, eating up everything on their way. Georgetown was abandoned; the monsters were in complete control.

"They will be cut off from the main herd," the optimistic reports announced. "We shall deal with the main herd first. This year the sacrifice will have to be made, but it will be the last. Scientists have at last hit upon an infallible toxin which will utterly destroy this menace within a few months."

Nobody believed that story, for everything had been tried and failed. In their laboratory Cliff and Kay were working frantically. And now the coldness that had developed between them was affecting their collaboration too. Cliff was keeping something back from Kay.

Kay knew it. Cliff had made some discovery that he was not sharing with his partner. Often Kay, entering the laboratory, would find Cliff furtively attempting to conceal some operation that he was in the midst of. Kay said nothing, but a brooding anger began to fill his heart. So Cliff was trying to get all the credit for the result of their years of work together!

And always, in the back of his mind, there was a vision of the little Government ticket in Ruth's hand, with the numbers in staring black type. They had burned into his brain. He could never forget them. Often at night, after a hard day's work, he would suddenly awaken out of a hideous nightmare, in which he saw Ruth taken away by the agents of the Government, to be thrown as a sacrifice to the monsters.

And Cliff was hiding something! That made the situation unbearable.

The coolness between the two men was rapidly changing into open animosity. And then one day, quite by chance, in Cliff's absence, Kay came upon evidence of Cliff's activities.

Cliff was no longer experimenting with the W-ray! He was using a new type of ray altogether, the next series, the psenium electron emanation discovered only a few years before, which had the peculiar property of non-alternation, even when the psenium electron changed its orbit around the central nucleus of the psenium atom.

Instead of discontinuity, the psenium electron had been found to emit radiation steadily, and this had upset the classic theories of matter for the ninth time in the past fifteen years.

And Kay's wrath broke loose in a storm of reproaches when Cliff came into the laboratory.

"You've been deliberately keeping me in the dark!" he shouted. "You're a nice sort of partner to have! Here's where we split up the combination, Hynes!"

"I've been thinking that for a long time," sneered Cliff. "The fact is, Kay, you're a little too elementary in your ideas to suit me. It's due to you that I kept hammering away on the wrong tack for years. The sooner we part, the better."

"No time like now," said Kay. "Keep your laboratory. You put most of the money into it, anyway. I'll build me another—where I can work without being hampered by a partner who's out for himself all the time. Good luck to you in your researches, and I hope you'll get all the credit when you find a way of annihilating the Earth Giants."

And he stormed out of the laboratory, jumped into his plane, and winged his way southward toward his apartment in New York.

Crowds in the streets of every town on the way. In villages and hamlets, swarming like ants, and hurrying along the highways! Kay, who flew one of the slow, old-fashioned planes, averaging little more than a hundred miles an hour, winged his way methodically overhead, too much absorbed in his anger against Cliff to pay much attention to this phenomenon at first. But gradually it was borne in upon him that something was wrong.

He flew lower, and now he was passing over a substantial town, and he could hear the shouts of anger that came up to him. The whole town was in a ferment, gathered in the town square.

Suddenly the reason came home to Kay. He saw the adjoining airport, and dropped like a plummet, hovering down until his wheels touched the ground. Without waiting to taxi into one of the public hangars, he leaped out and ran through the deserted grounds into the square.

Groans, yells, shrieks of derision rent the air. The whole crowd had gone maniacal. And it was as Kay had thought. Upon a white background high up on the town ball building, the numbers of the local boys and girls who had been picked for sacrifices were being shown.

Eight boys and fifteen girls, already on their way into the wastes of South America, to meet a hideous death.

"They took my Sally," screamed a wizened woman, the tears raining down her checks. "Kidnapped her at the street corner after dark. I didn't know why she hadn't come home last night. God, my Sally, my little girl, gone—gone—"

"People, you must be patient," boomed the Government announcer. "The President feels with you in your affliction. But by next year a means will have been devised of destroying these monsters. Your children will have their sacrifice recorded in the Hall of Fame. They are true soldiers who—"

"To hell with the Government!" roared a man. "Stop that damn talk machine! Break her, fellows! Then we'll hang President Bogart from the top of the Capitol!"

Yells answered him, and the crowd surged forward toward the building.

"Stand back!" shrieked the announcer. "It's death to set foot on the step. We are now electrified. Last warning!"

The first ranks of the mob recoiled as a charge of electricity at a voltage just short of that required to take life coursed through their bodies. Shrieks of agony rang out. Files of writhing forms covered the ground.

Kay rushed to the automatic clerk at the window beside the metal steps, taking care to avoid contact with them. Within six feet, the temperature of his body brought the thermostatic control into action; the window slid upward and the dummy appeared. He turned the dial to Albany.

"I want New York Division, Sub-station F, Loyalist Registration," he called. "Give me Z numbers of the lottery, please."

"No numbers will be given out until Horometer 13," the dummy boomed.

"But I tell you I must know immediately!" Kay pleaded frantically.

"Stand away, please!"

"I've got to know, I tell you!"

"We are now electrified. Last warning!"

"Listen to me. My name's Kay Bevan. I—"

A mighty buffet in the chest hurled Kay ten feet backward upon the ground. He rose, came within the electric zone, felt his arms twisted in a giant's grasp, staggered back again and sat down gasping. The window went down noiselessly, the dummy swung back into place. Kay got upon his feet again, choking with impotent rage.

All about him men and women were milling in a frantic mob. He broke through them, went back to where his plane was standing. A minute later he was driving madly toward the district airport in New York within three blocks of Ruth's apartment.

He dropped into a vacant landing place, checked hastily, and rushed into the elevator. Once in the upper street, he bounded to the middle platform, and, not satisfied to let it convey him at eight miles an hour, strode on through the indignant throng until he reached his destination. Hurling the crowds right and left he gained the exit, and a half-minute later was on the upper level of the apartment block.

He pushed past the janitor and raced along the corridor to Ruth's apartment. She would be in if all was well; she worked for the Broadcast Association, correcting the proofs that came from the district headquarters by pneumatic tube. He stopped outside the door. The little dial of white light showed him that the apartment was unoccupied.

As he stood there in a daze, hoping against hope, he saw a thread hanging from the crevice between door and frame. He pulled at it, and drew out a tiny strip of scandium, the new compressible metal that had become fashionable for engagement rings. Plastic, all but invisible, it could be compressed to the thickness of a sheet of paper: it was the token of secret lovers, and Kay had given Ruth a ring of it.

It was the signal, the dreaded signal that Ruth had been on the lottery list—the only signal that she had been able to convey, since stringent precautions were taken to prevent the victims becoming known until all possibility of rescue was removed.

No chance of rescuing her! From a hundred airports the great Government airships had long since sailed into the skies, carrying those selected by the wheel at Washington for sacrifice to the Earth Giants. Only one chance remained. If Cliff had discovered the secret that had so long eluded them, surely he would reveal it to him now!

Their quarrel was forgotten. Kay only knew that the woman he loved was even then speeding southward to be thrown to the maw of the vile monsters that held the world in terror. Surely Cliff would bend every effort to save her!

Only a few hours had passed since Kay had stormed out of the laboratory in the Adirondacks in a rage when he was back on their little private landing field. He leaped from the plane and ran up the trail beside the lake between the trees. The cabin was dark; and, when Kay reached the laboratory he found it dark too.

"Cliff! Cliff!" he shouted.

No answer came, and with a sinking heart he snapped the button at the door. It failed to throw the expected flood of light through the interior. With shaking hand Kay pulled the little electron torch from his pocket, and its bright beam showed that the door was padlocked. He moved round to the window. The glass was unbreakable, but the ray from the torch showed that the interior of the laboratory had been dismantled, and the great top was gone.

In those few hours Cliff, for reasons best known to himself, had removed the top, Kay's one hope of saving Ruth. And he was gone.

In that moment Kay went insane. He raved and cursed, calling down vengeance upon Cliff's head. Cliff's very motive was incredible. That he had deliberately removed the top in order that Ruth should die was not, of course, conceivable. But in that first outburst of fury Kay did not consider that.

Presently Kay's madness burned itself out. There was still one thing that he could do. His plane, slow though it was, would carry him to the pampas. He could get fresh fuel at numerous bootleg petrol stations, even though the regulations against intersectional flight were rigid. With luck he could reach the pampas, perhaps before the sluggish monsters had fallen upon their prey. It was said that the victims sometimes waited for days!

Something was rubbing against his leg, pricking it through his anklets. Kay looked down. A lady porcupine, with tiny new quills, was showing recognition, even affection, if such a spiny beast could be said to possess that quality.

Somehow the presence of the beast restored Kay's mind to normal.

"Well, he's left us both in the lurch, Susie," he said. "Good luck to you, beastie, and may you find a secure hiding place until your quills have grown."

Drowning men catch at straws. Kay snatched out his watch, and the illuminated dial showed that it was already two quintets past horometer 13. He darted back to the cabin. The door was unfastened, and his torch showed him that, though Cliff had evidently departed, and taken his things, the interior was much as it had been. When Kay picked up the telephotophone, the oblong dial flashed out. The instrument was in working order.

He turned the crank, and swiftly a succession of scenes flashed over the dial. On this little patch of glassite, Kay was actually making the spatial journey to Albany, each minutest movement of the crank representing a distance covered. The building of the New York Division appeared, and its appearance signified that Kay was telephonically connected. But there was no automatic voice attachment, an expense that Kay and Cliff had decided would be unjustified. He had to rely upon the old-fashioned telephone, such as was still widely in use in rural districts. He took up the receiver.

"Sub-Station F, Loyalist Registration, please," he called.

"Speaking," said a girl's voice presently.

"I want the Z numbers. All from Z5 to ZA," said Kay.

And thus, in the dark hut, he listened to the doom pronounced, miles away, by a more or less indifferent operator. When the fatal number was read out, he thanked her and hung up. He released the crank, which moved back to its position, putting out the light on the dial.

For a moment or two he stood there motionless, in a sort of daze, though actually he was gathering all his reserves of resolution for the task confronting him. Simply to find Ruth among the hundred thousand victims, and die with her. A task stupendous in itself, and yet Kay had no doubt that he would succeed, that he would be holding her in his arms when the tide of hell flowed over them.

He knew the manner of that death. The irresistible onset of the giant masses of protoplasm, the extrusion of temporary arms, or feelers, that would grasp them, drag them into the heart of the yielding substance, and slowly smother them to death while the life was drained from their bodies. It had been said the death was painless, but that was Government propaganda. But he would be holding Ruth in his arms. He'd find her: he had no doubt of that at all.

And, strangely enough, now that Kay knew the worst, now that not the slightest doubt remained, he was conscious of an elevation of spirits, a sort of mad recklessness that was perfectly indefinable.

Kay turned his torch into a corner of the kitchen. Yes, there was the thing subconsciousness had prompted him to seek. A long-shafted, heavy woodsman's ax, a formidable weapon at close quarters. Because it is the instinct of *homo Americanus* to die with a weapon in his hands, rather than let himself be butchered helplessly, Kay snatched it up. He ran back to his plane.

The gas tank was nearly empty, but there was petrol in the ice house beside the lake.

Kay wheeled the machine up to it, and filled up with gas and oil. All ready now! He leaped in, pressed the starter, soared vertically, helicopter wings fluttering like a soaring hawk's. Up to the passenger air lane at nine thousand: higher to twelve, the track of the international and supply ships; higher still, to the fourteen thousand ceiling of the antiquated machine. He banked, turned southward.

It was freezing cold up there, and Kay had no flying suit on him, but, between the passenger lane and the lane of the heliospheres, at thirty thousand, there was no air police. And he could afford to take no chances. The Government police would be on the lookout for a score such desperate men as he, bent on a similar mission. He drove the plane toward the Atlantic till a red glow began to diffuse itself beneath him, an area of conflagration covering square miles of territory.

Swooping lower, Kay could hear the sound of detonations, the roar of old-fashioned guns, while through the pall of lurid smoke came the long, violet flashes of atomic guns, cleaving lanes of devastation. New York was burning.

The frenzied populace had broken into revolt, seized the guns stored in the arsenals, and attacked the great Bronx fortress that stood like a mighty sentinel to protect the port.

A swarm of airships came into view, swirling in savage fight. Kay zoomed. It was not his battle.

Now New York lay behind him, and he was winging southward over the Atlantic. All night he flew. At dawn he came down in a coast hamlet for bootleg petrol and oil.

"You come from New York?" asked the Georgian. "Hear there's war broke out up there."

"My war's down in Brazil," muttered Kay.

"Say, if them Giants comes up here yuh know what us folks is going to do? We're going to set the hounds on 'em. Yes, sirree, we've got a pack of bloodhounds, raised for jest that purpose. I guess that's something them wisecrackers at Washington ain't thought of. They took two little fellers from Hopetown, but they won't take nobody from here."

Kay fuelled up and resumed his flight southward.

After that it was a nightmare. The sun rose and set, alternating with the staring moon and stars. Kay crossed the Caribbean, sighted the South American coast, swept southward over the jungles of Brazil. He drank, but no food passed his lips. He had become a mechanism, set for on special purpose—self-immolation.

It was in a wide savannah among the jungles that he first caught sight of the monsters. At first he thought it was the rising dawn mist; then he began to distinguish a certain horrible resemblance to human forms, and swooped down, banking round and round the opening in the jungle until he could see clearly.

There were perhaps a score of them, an advance guard that had pushed forward from one of the main divisions. Men? Anthropoids, rather, for their sex was indistinguishable! Human forms ranging from a few feet to a hundred, composed apparently of a grayish jelly, propelling themselves clumsily on two feet, but floating rather than walking. Translucent, semi-transparent. Most horrible of all, these shadowy, spheroid creatures exhibited here and there buds of various sizes, which were taking on the similitude of fresh forms. And among them were the young, the buds that had fallen from the parent stems, fully formed humans of perhaps five or six feet, bouncing with a horrible playfulness among their sires.

As Kay soared some three hundred feet overhead, a young tapir came leaping out of the jungle and ran, apparently unconscious of their presence, right toward the monsters. Suddenly it stopped, and Kay saw that it was already encircled by coils of protoplasm, resembling arms, which had shot forth from the bodies of the devils.

Swiftly, despite its struggles and bleatings, the tapir was drawn into the substance of the monsters, which seemed to fuse together and form a solid wall of protoplasm in all respects like the agglutination of bacteria under certain conditions.

Then the beast vanished in the wall, whose agitated churnings alone gave proof of its existence.

For perhaps ten minutes longer Kay remained hovering above the clearing. Then the bodies divided, resuming their separate shapes. And the white bones of the tapir lay in a huddled mass in the open.

Kay went mad. Deliberately he set down his plane, and, hatchet in hand, advanced upon the sluggish monsters. Shouting wildly, he leaped into their midst.

The fight that followed was like a nightmare fight. He lopped off the slow tentacles that sought to envelop him, he slashed the devils into long ribbons of writhing jelly, slashed until the substance blunted the ax; wiped it clean and leaped into their midst again, hewing until he could no longer raise his arm. Then he drew back and surveyed the scene before him.

It was dreadful enough to drive the last remnants of sanity from his brain. For every piece that he had cut from the monsters, every protoplasmic ribbon was reorganizing before his eyes into the semblance of a new creature. Where there had been a score, there were now five hundred!

Kay ran back to his plane, leaped in, and soared southward. His face was a grotesque mask of madness, and his cries rang out through the ether.

The victims were no longer chained to stakes. The Federation, which always acted with complete secrecy, had gone one better. It had engaged electrical engineers, kept them housed in secret places, transported them to Golgotha; and there a vast electrified field had been established, an open space whose boundaries were marked out by pillars of electron steel.

Between these pillars ran lines of electric force. To attempt to pass them meant—not death, for dead boys and girls were spurned by the devils—but a violent shock that hurled one backward.

On this great plain the hundred thousand victims sat huddled in the open. Food they had none, for no purpose was to be served by mitigating their last agonies. No shelter either, for the sight of buildings might delay the final phase. But high above the doomed there floated the flag of the Federation, on a lofty pole, a touch of ironic sentimentality that had commended itself to some mind at Washington.

Over a square mile of territory, ringed with jungle the victims lay. The majority of them ringed this terrain; that is to say, attempting to escape, they had been hurled back by the electrical charge, and, having no strength or will remaining, they had dropped where they had been hurled, and lay in apathetic resignation.

There had been screams and cries for mercy, and piteous scenes when the Government airships had deposited them there and flown away, but now an intense silence had descended upon the doomed. Resigned to their fate, they sat or lay in little silent groups, all eyes turned toward the gloomy jungle.

And everywhere within this jungle a wraith-like mist was forming at this dawn hour. From a thousand miles around, the devils were mustering for their prey, agglutinating, in order that the meal of one might become the meal of all.

Wisps of protoplasmic fog were stealing out through the trees, changing shape every instant, but always advancing: now presenting the appearance of an aligned regiment of huge, shadowy men, now nothing but a wall of semi-solid vapor. And still, with eyeballs straining in their sockets, the victims watched.

Suddenly all were seized with the same spasm of mad terror. Again they hurled themselves against the electrified lines, and again they were hurled back, masses of boys and girls tumbling against one another, and screaming in one wail that, could it have been heard in Washington, would have driven all insane. Again and again, till they fell back, panting and helpless. And solidly the wall of devils was creeping up from every side.

Ruth Deane, one of the few who had themselves in control, lay some distance back from the electrified field. From the moment when she was surprised in her apartment by the Government representatives, she had known that there was no hope of escape.

She had slipped the ring off her finger, snapped the plastic metal, and attached it to a thread torn from her dress. She had managed to insert it in the door, hoping that Kay would find it. It would serve as a last message of love to him.

Every removal of a selected victim was in the nature of a kidnapping. At dead of night her apartment had been opened. She had been ordered to dress. Nothing could be written, no arrangements made. She was already considered as one dead.

She had been hurried out of the upper entrance to the monorail, which conveyed her in a special car to the landing station. A few minutes later she had been on her way to join the camp of other victims, a hundred miles away. Within two hours she was on her way southward.

Stunned by the tragedy, none of the victims had made much of an outcry. They had been given water by the airship police. No food for boys and girls already dead. Days and nights had passed, and now she was here, faint from exhaustion, and wondering at the despair shown by those others. What difference would it make in half an hour? Besides, that Government pamphlet had insisted that this death was painless!

But an immense longing to see Kay once more came over her. There had been a time when she thought she loved Cliff; then Kay had come into her life, and she had known that other affair was folly. She had never told Kay of the bitter scene between Cliff and herself, how he had raved against Kay and sworn to win her in the end.

Cliff had calmed down and apologized, and Ruth had never seen him again. She wished he had not taken it like that. But above all she wanted to see Kay, just to say good-by.

And she tried to send out her whole heart to him in an unspoken message of love that would surely somehow convey itself to him.

The wall of devils was creeping up on every side, slowly, lethargically. The monsters took their time, because they knew they were invincible. The sobs and shrieks had died away. Collected into a mass almost as rigid as that of the Earth Giants, the victims waited, palsied as a rabbit that awaits the approach of the serpent.

A humming overhead. An airplane shooting down from the sky. Rescue? No. Only a solitary pilot, armed with a woodsman's ax.

Kay drifted down, touched ground, leaped to his feet. Chance had brought him within five hundred yards of where Ruth was standing. But Ruth had known who that lone flyer must be. She broke through the throng; she rushed to meet him. Her arms were around him.

"Kay, darling Kay!"

"Ruth, dearest!"

"I knew you'd come."

"I've come to die beside you!"

It was perhaps odd that it did not enter the head of either as a possibility that Kay should simply place Ruth in the plane and fly away with here to safety. Had the thought occurred to Kay, he might have been tempted. But such black treachery was something inconceivable by either. So long as the Federation remained, so long as man moved in an organized society, he was bound to his fellows, to fight, suffer, and die with them.

"Stand by me, Ruth. We're going down fighting."

They moved back toward the throng, which, momentarily stirred to hope by Kay's appearance, had fallen into the former apathy of despair. And now the monsters were beginning to enter the electrified zone at one point. As they passed the line of posts, the high tension current made their bodies luminous, but it had no appreciable effect upon them. They moved on, inevitably.

A score or so of semi-human forms, agglutinated into a mass, and yet individually discernible. They bore down slowly upon the crowd of victims, who pressed backward as they advanced. On the other sides, though they almost encircled the field of death, the monsters were making no maneuvers to entrap their prey. Their sluggish minds were incapable of conceiving anything of the kind. But for the electrified zone, the great majority of the victims could have effected their escape. The monsters were simply pressing forward to their meal; they did not interpret its capture in terms of strategy at all.

A new frenzy of horror seized the crowd. They fled, struggling back until the foremost in flight reached the other side of Golgotha, to be repulsed by the electrified zone there. They fell in tumbled heaps. Appalling shrieks rang through the air.

Another line of the monsters was seeping forward, converging toward the first. As the two lines met, they coalesced into a wall of protoplasm, a thousand feet in length by a hundred high. A wall out of which leered phantasmal faces, like those in a frieze.

Kay stood alone, his arm around Ruth. To follow the flying mob would but prolong the agony. He raised the ax. He looked into the girl's eyes. She understood, and nodded.

One last embrace, one kiss, and Kay placed her behind him. He sprang forward, shouting, and plunged into the very heart of the wall.

And Ruth, watching with eyes dilated with horror, saw it yield with a sucking sound, and saw Kay disappear within it.

She saw the hideous mass fold itself upon him, and a hundred extruded tentacles wave in the air as they blindly grappled for him. And then Kay had broken through, and was hewing madly with great sweeps of the ax that slashed great streamers of the amorphous tissue from the wall of protoplasm.

It recoiled and then folded once more, and Kay's mighty sweeps were slashing phantom limbs from phantom bodies; and lopping off tentacles that curled and coiled, and put forth caricatures of hands and fingers, and then, uniting with other slashed off tentacles, began to mould themselves into the likeness of dwarf monsters. Kay's struggle was like that of a man fighting a fog, for again and again he broke through the wall, and always it reunited.

And behind it another wall of protoplasm was pressing forward, and on another side a wall was drifting up. As Kay stopped, panting, and momentarily free, Ruth saw that they were almost encircled.

She saw the nature of that fight. Inevitably that wall would close about them; and, though the bones of last year's victims had been gathered up and carried away by the Federation, she guessed what would occur.

She ran to Kay and dragged him back through the closing gap. It met behind them, and again they stood face to face with the devils. Only this time, instead of a wall of protoplasm, it was a veritable mountain that confronted them, and there could be no more breaking through.

Kay thought afterward that the one touch of absolute horror was that the reforming monsters, the young ones growing visibly before his eyes, had the gamboling instinct of young lambs or other creatures. They were much more lively than the parent creatures.

By this time perhaps a third of the space within the electrified lines had been occupied by the devils. The wall was slowly and sluggishly advancing, and a fresh infiltration was drifting in on another side. As the victims were pressed closer and closer together in their flight, half of them seemed to go insane. They raced to and fro, laughing and screaming, flinging their arms aloft in extravagant gestures. One young fellow, rushing across the ground, hurled himself like a bolt from a catapult into the heart of the grisly mass, which opened and received him.

There was a struggle, a convulsion; then the mass moved on.

Kay wiped his ax. He stood beside Ruth, gathering strength and breath to fight again. What else was there to do?

Suddenly a humming sound came to his ears. Still some little distance from the monsters, he glanced back. The victims were shouting, staring upward. Over the tops of the jungle trees Kay saw a second airplane flying toward them, a larger one than the plane which he had flown.

It opened its helicopter wings and drifted downward. Kay saw a single pilot, and, in the baggage compartment something that at first he did not recognize. Then he recognized both this object and the aviator.

"It's Cliff," he whispered hoarsely. "He's brought the top!"

The crowd was milling about Cliff as he stepped out of the plane. Kay broke through their midst, shouting to them to clear a space, that it was their chance, their only chance. They heard him and obeyed. And Cliff and Kay clasped hands, and there was Ruth beside them.

The two men carried the top out of the baggage compartment and set it up.

"Thank God I came in time," Cliff hissed. "How long have we got, Kay?"

"Five minutes, I think," Kay answered, glancing at the oncoming wall. "They're slow. Will it work, Cliff? God, when I found you'd gone last night—"

Cliff did not answer. Ignoring Kay's offer of assistance, he fitted the top tightly into its socket of craolite, much heavier than the former one. Beneath this, three heavy craolite legs formed a sort of tripod.

"I looked forward to this possibility, Kay," said Cliff, as he adjusted the top and turned the clamps that held it in position. "Sorry I had to deceive you, but you we're so set on the cosmic rays, and I knew the psenium emanations wouldn't appeal to you. You wouldn't have believed. I had a hunch Ruth would draw one of those numbers.... *How long?*"

The swaying masses of gray jelly were very near them. Cliff worked feverishly at the top.

"Let me help. Cliff!"

"No! I'm through! Stand back!" shouted Cliff.

Even then—he regretted it afterward, and knew that he would regret it to his dying day—even then the thought flashed through Kay's mind that Cliff wanted all the glory. Behind him the milling, screaming crowd was huddling, as if for protection. Slowly a wisp-like tentacle protruded from the advancing wall. Kay swung his ax and lopped it from the phantom body. But the wall was almost upon them, and from the other side it was advancing rapidly.

"I'm ready! Stand back!" Cliff turned upon Kay, his face white, his voice hoarse. "I've one request to make, Kay. Keep everybody back, including you and Ruth. Nobody is to come within twenty-five yards of this machine!"

"That shall be done," said Kay, a little bitterness in his tone.

"Ruth, I think I'm going to save you all." Cliff looked into the girl's face for a moment. "Please stand back twenty-five yards," he repeated.

Kay took Ruth by the arm and drew her back. The crowd moved back, their pressure moving back the vast multitudes behind them. The vast mob was almost packed into the quarter of the Golgotha; there was scarcely room to move.

Kay saw Cliff press the lever.

Slowly the giant top began to whirl. Faster ... faster.... Now it was revolving so fast that it had become totally invisible. But Cliff was almost surrounded by the wall of jelly. Only his back could be seen, and then space was narrowing fast.

Kay gripped Ruth's arm tightly. He held his breath. The crowd, of whom only a small part knew what was taking place, was screaming with terror as the mass of jelly on the other side pressed them inexorably backward. And Cliff had almost vanished. Would the machine work? Was it possible that the psenium emanations would succeed where the Millikan rays, the W-ray had failed?

Then of a sudden the air grew dark as night. Kay began to sneeze. He gasped for air. He was choking. He could see nothing, and he strained Ruth to him convulsively, while the terrified multitudes behind him set up a last wail of despair.

He could see nothing, and he stood with the ax ready for the onset of the monsters, more terrible now, in their invisibility, than before. Then of a sudden there sounded subterranean rumblings. The ground seemed to open almost under Kay's feet.

He leaped back, dragging Ruth with him. Slowly the dust was settling, the darkness lessening. A faint, luminous glow overhead revealed the sun. Kay was aware that Cliff had swung the top, so that the psenium rays were being brought to bear upon the second mass of the monsters on the other side.

The sun vanished in appalling blackness. Again the dust-choked air was almost unbreathable. The shrieks of the crowd died away in wheezing gasps; and then a wilder clamor began.

"The earthquake! The earthquake!" a girl was shrilling. "God help us all!"

Kay stood still, clutching Ruth tightly in his arms. He dared not stir, for all the world seemed to be dissolving into chaos.

Slowly the dust began to settle again. Perhaps five minutes passed before the sunbeams began to struggle through. A cloud of grey dust still obscured everything. But the wall of protoplasm was gone!

Cliff's voice came moaning out of the murk, calling Kay's name.

Kay moved forward cautiously, still holding Ruth. He seemed to be skirting the edge of a vast crater. At the edge of it he found the top, revolving slowly. And Cliff's voice came from beside the top.

"Kay, we've won. Don't look at me. Don't let Ruth see me! Look down!"

Kay looked down into the bottomless pit, extending clear across the plain to the distant jungle. An enormous canyon cloven in the earth, filled with the slowly settling cloud of dust.

"They're there, Kay. Don't look this way!"

But Kay looked—and could see nothing except a pile of debris, from the bottom of which Cliff's voice issued.

"Cliff, you're not hurt?"

"A—a little. You must listen while I tell you how to clean up the monsters. It's the psenium emanation. It has the same effect when our method is applied to it. It disintegrates everything inorganic—not organic.

"I thought, if I couldn't get them, I'd crumble the earth away—bury them. They're underneath the debris, Kay, a mile deep, buried, beneath the impalpable powder that represented the inorganic salts and minerals of the earth. They'll never get out of that. Protoplasm needs oxygen. They'll trouble us no more.

"You must take the top, Kay. Use our old method. You'll find its application to the psenium emanation written in a book fastened beneath the hood. Wipe out the rest of them. If any more come, you'll know how to deal with them."

"Cliff, you're not badly hurt?" Kay asked again.

"Don't look, I tell you! Keep Ruth away!"

But the dust was settling fast, and suddenly Ruth uttered a scream of fear.

And a strangled cry broke from Kay's throat as he looked down at what had been Cliff Hynes.

The man seemed to have become resolved into the same sort of protoplasm as the Earth Giants. He lay, a little heap, incredibly small, incredibly distorted. Flesh without bones, shapeless lumps of flesh where arms and legs and body frame should have been.

Cliff's voice came faintly. "You remember the leakage through the rubber and analektron container, Kay. The W-rays even fused the craolite socket. The psenium rays are stronger. They destroy even bone. They're fatal to the man who operates the machine, unless he follows the directions. I've written them out for you, but I had—no time—to apply them."

His voice broke off. Then, "Good luck to you and—Ruth, Kay," he whispered, absent inaudibly. "Don't let—her—look at me."

Kay led Ruth gently away. "Did you hear that?" she whispered, sobbing. "He died to save us Kay."

It was like a return from the grave for the amazed boys and girls who—since the onset of the monsters had destroyed the electric lines—poured out of the plain of Golgotha to life and freedom.

Many of them had gone mad, a few had died of fright, but the rest would come back to normal, and the world was saved.

Hunger was their greatest problem, for, despite Kay's hurried flight to the nearest occupied post, it was difficult to convince the Federation officials that the devils were really gone, buried beneath a mile of crumbled earth. And Kay had to be back to mop up other, smaller bands that had spread through the forests.

It was six months before the last of the monsters had been obliterated, and then Kay, now one of the highest officials in the Federation's service, was granted a lunarian's leave of absence pending his taking command of an Antarctic expedition for the purpose of destroying the remaining monsters in their lair.

He took this opportunity to be married to Ruth, in the church in his native town, which was *en fête* for the occasion.

"Thinking of Cliff?" Kay asked his bride, as she settled in his plane preparatory to their starting for the honeymoon in the Adirondacks. "I think he would be happy if he knew. He saved the world, dear; he gave his best. And that was all he wanted."

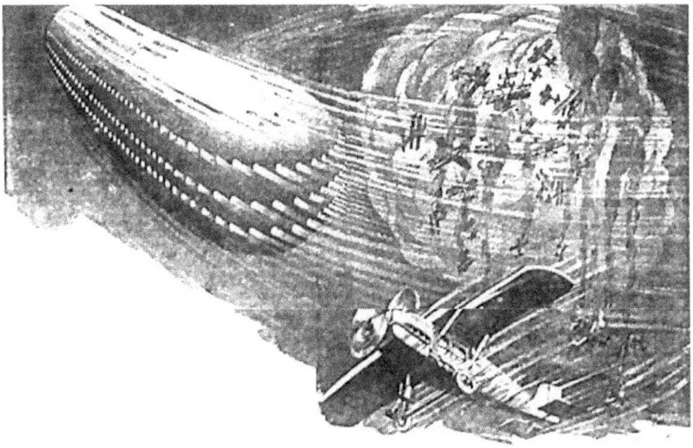

THE PIRATE PLANET

BEGINNING A FOUR-PART NOVEL

By Charles W. Diffin

Like rats in a cage, the planes of the 91st Squadron were darting and whirling.

CHAPTER I

Lieutenant McGuire threw open his coat with its winged insignia of the air force and leaned back in his chair to read more comfortably the newspaper article.

A strange light blinks on Venus, and over old Earth hovers a mysterious visitant—dread harbinger of interplanetary war.

He glanced at Captain Blake across the table. The captain was deep in a game of solitaire, but he looked up at McGuire's audible chuckle.

"Gay old girl!" said Lieutenant McGuire and smoothed the paper across his knees. "She's getting flirtatious."

The captain swore softly as he gathered up his cards. "Not interested," he announced; "too hot to-night. Keep her away."

"Oh, she's far enough away," McGuire responded; "about seventy million miles. Don't get excited."

"What are you talking about?" The captain shuffled his cards irritably.

"Venus. She's winking at us, the old reprobate. One of these star-gazers up on Mount Lawson saw the flashes a week or so ago. If you'll cut out your solitaire and listen, I'll read you something to improve your mind." He ignored the other's disrespectful remark and held the paper closer to see the paragraphs.

"Is Venus Signalling?" inquired the caption which Lieutenant McGuire read. "Professor Sykes of Mt. Lawson Observatory Reports Flashes.

"The planet Venus, now a brilliant spectacle in the evening sky, is behaving strangely according to a report from the local observatory on Mount Lawson. This sister star, most like Earth of all the planets, is now at its eastern elongation, showing like a half-moon in the big telescopes on Mt. Lawson. Shrouded in impenetrable clouds, its surface has never been seen, but something is happening there. Professor Sykes reports seeing a distinct flash of light upon the terminator, or margin of light. It lasted for several seconds and was not repeated.

"No explanation of the phenomenon is offered by scientists, as conditions on the planet's surface are unknown. Is there life there? Are the people of Venus trying to communicate? One guess is as good as another. But it is interesting to recall that our scientists recently proposed to send a similar signal from Earth to Mars by firing a tremendous flare of magnesium.

"Venus is now approaching the earth; she comes the nearest of all planets. Have the Venusians penetrated their cloak of cloud masses with a visible light? The planet will be watched with increased interest as it swings toward us in space, in hope of there being a repetition of the unexplained flash."

"There," said Lieutenant McGuire,"—doesn't that elevate your mind? Take it off this infernally hot night? Carry you out through the cool reaches of interplanetary space? If there is anything else you want to know, just ask me."

"Yes," Captain Blake agree, "there is. I want to know how the game came out back in New York—and you don't know that. Let's go over and ask the radio man. He probably has the dope."

"Good idea," said McGuire; "maybe he has picked up a message from Venus; we'll make a date." He looked vainly for the brilliant star as they walked out into the night. There were clouds of fog from the nearby Pacific drifting high overhead. Here and there stars showed momentarily, then were blotted from sight.

The operator in the radio room handed the captain a paper with the day's scores from the eastern games. But Lieutenant McGuire, despite his ready amusement at the idea, found his thoughts clinging to the words he had read. "Was the planet communicating?" he pictured the great globe—another Earth—slipping silently through space, coming nearer and nearer.

Did they have radio? he wondered. Would they send recognizable signals—words—or some mathematical sequence to prove their reality? He turned to the radio operator on duty.

"Have you picked up anything peculiar," he asked, and laughed inwardly at himself for the asking. "Any new dots and dashes? The scientists say that Venus is calling. You'll have to be learning a new code."

The man glanced at him strangely and looked quickly away.

"No, sir," he said. And added after a pause: "No new dots and dashes."

"Don't take that stuff too seriously, Mac," the captain remonstrated. "The day of miracles is past; we don't want to commit you to the psychopathic ward. Now here is something real: the Giants won, and I had ten dollars on them. How shall we celebrate?"

The radio man was listening intently as they started to leave. His voice was hesitating as he stopped them; he seemed reluctant to put his thoughts into words.

"Just a minute, sir," he said to Captain Blake.

"Well?" the captain asked. And again the man waited before he replied. Then—

"Lieutenant McGuire asked me," he began, "if I had heard any strange dots and dashes. I have not; but ... well, the fact is, sir, that I have been getting some mighty queer sounds for the past few nights. They've got me guessing.

"If you wouldn't mind waiting. Captain; they're about due now—" He listened again to some signal inaudible to the others, then hooked up two extra head-sets for the officers.

"It's on now," he said. "If you don't mind—"

McGuire grinned at the captain as they took up the ear-phones. "Power of suggestion," he whispered, but the smile was erased from his lips as he listened. For in his ear was sounding a weird and wailing note.

No dots or dashes, as the operator had said, but the signal was strong. It rose and fell and wavered into shrill tremolos, a ghostly, unearthly sound, and it kept on and on in a shrill despairing wail. Abruptly it stopped.

The captain would have removed the receiver from his ear, but the operator stopped him. "Listen," he said, "to the answer."

There was silence, broken only by an occasional hiss and crackle of some far distant mountain storm. Then, faint as a whisper, came an answering, whistling breath.

It, too, trembled and quavered. It went up—up—to the limit of hearing; then slid down the scale to catch and tremble and again ascend in endless unvarying ups and downs of sound. It was another unbroken, unceasing, but always changing vibration.

"What in thunder is that?" Captain Blake demanded.

"Communication of some sort, I should say," McGuire said slowly, and he caught the operator's eyes upon him in silent agreement.

"No letters," Blake objected; "no breaks; just that screech." He listened again. "Darned if it doesn't almost seem to say something," he admitted.

"When did you first hear this?" he demanded of the radio man.

"Night before last, sir. I did not report it. It seemed too—too—"

"Quite so," said Captain Blake in understanding, "but it is some form of broadcasting on a variable wave; though how a thing like that can make sense—"

"They talk back and forth," said the operator; "all night, most. Notice the loud one and the faint one; two stations sending and answering."

Captain Blake waved him to silence. "Wait—wait!" he ordered. "It's growing louder!"

In the ears of the listening men the noise dropped to a loud grumble; rose to a piercing shriek; wavered and leaped rapidly from note to note. It was increasing; rushing upon them with unbearable sound. The sense of something approaching, driving toward them swiftly, was strong upon Lieutenant McGuire. He tore the head-phones from his ears and rushed to the door. The captain was beside him. Whoever—whatever—was sending that mysterious signal was coming near—but was that nearness a matter of miles or of thousands of miles?

They stared at the stormy night sky above. A moon was glowing faintly behind scudding clouds, and the gray-black of flying shadows formed an opening as they watched, a wind-blown opening like a doorway to the infinity beyond, where, blocking out the stars, was a something that brought a breath-catching shout from the watching men.

Some five thousand feet up in the night was a gleaming ship. There were rows of portholes that shone twinkling against the black sky—portholes in multiple rows on the side. The craft was inconceivably huge. Formless and dim of outline in the darkness, its vast bulk was unmistakable.

And as they watched with staring, incredulous eyes, it seemed to take alarm as if it sensed the parting of its concealing cloud blanket. It shot with dizzy speed and the roar of a mighty meteor straight up into the night. The gleam of its twinkling lights merged to a distant star that dwindled, shrank and vanished in the heights.

The men were wordless and open-mouthed. They stared at each other in disbelief of what their eyes had registered.

"A liner!" gasped Captain Blake. "A—a—liner! Mac, there is no such thing."

McGuire pointed where the real cause of their visitor's departure appeared. A plane with engine wide open came tearing down through the clouds. It swung in a great spiral down over the field and dropped a white flare as it straightened away; then returned for the landing. It taxied at reckless speed toward the hangars and stopped a short distance from the men. The pilot threw himself out of the cockpit and raced drunkenly toward them.

"Did you see it?" he shouted, his voice a cracked scream. "Did you see it?"

"We saw it," said Captain Blake; "yes, we saw it. Big as—" He sought vainly for a proper comparison, then repeated his former words: "Big as an ocean liner!"

The pilot nodded; he was breathing heavily.

"Any markings?" asked his superior. "Anything to identify it?"

"Yes, there were markings, but I don't know what they mean. There was a circle painted on her bow and marks like clouds around it, but I didn't have time to see much. I came out of a cloud, and there the thing was. I was flying at five thousand, and they hung there dead ahead. I couldn't believe it; it was monstrous; tremendous. Then they sighted me, I guess, and they up-ended that ship in mid-air and shot straight up till they were out of sight."

It was the captain's turn to nod mutely.

"There's your miracle," said Lieutenant McGuire softly.

"Miracle is right," agreed Captain Blake; "nothing less! But it is no miracle of ours, and I am betting it doesn't mean any good to us. Some other country has got the jump on us."

To the pilot he ordered: "Say nothing of this—not a word—get that? Let me have a written report: full details, but concise as possible."

He went back to the radio room, and the operator there received the same instructions.

"What are you going to do?" the lieutenant questioned.

Captain Blake was reaching for a head-set. "Listen in," he said briefly; "try to link up that impossible ship with those messages, then report at once to the colonel and whoever he calls in. I'll want you along, Mac, to swear I am sober."

He had a head-set adjusted, and McGuire took up the other. Again the room was still, and again from the far reaches of space the dark night sent to them its quavering call.

The weird shrillness cried less loudly now, and the men listened in strained silence to the go and come of that variable shriek. Musical at times as it leaped from one clear note to another, again it would merge into discordant blendings of half-tones that sent shivers of nervous reaction up the listeners' spines.

"Listen," said McGuire abruptly. "Check me on this. There are two of them, one loud and one faint—right?"

"Right," said Captain Blake.

"Now notice the time intervals—there! The faint one stops, and the big boy cuts in immediately. No waiting; he answers quickly. He does it every time."

"Well?" the captain asked.

"Listen when he stops and see how long before the faint one answers. Call the loud one the ship and the faint one the station.... There! The ship is through!"

There was pause; some seconds elapsed before the answer that whispered so faintly in their ears came out of the night.

"You are right, sir," the operator said in corroboration of McGuire's remark. "There is that wait every time."

"The ship answers at once," said McGuire; "the station only after a wait."

"Meaning—?" inquired the captain.

"Meaning, as I take it, that there is time required for the message to go from the ship to the station and for them to reply."

"An appreciable time like that," Captain Blake exclaimed, "—with radio! Why, a few seconds, even, would carry it around the world a score of times!"

Lieutenant McGuire hesitated a moment. "It happens every time," he reminded the captain: "it is no coincidence. And if that other station is out in space—another ship perhaps, relaying the messages to yet others between here and—Venus, let us say...."

He left the thought unfinished. Captain Blake was staring at him as one who beholds a fellow-man suddenly insane. But the look in his eyes changed slowly, and his lips that had been opened in remonstrance came gradually in a firm, straight line.

"Crazy!" he said, but it was apparent that he was speaking as much to himself as to McGuire. "Plumb, raving crazy!... Yet that ship *did* go straight up out of sight—an acceleration in the upper air beyond anything we know. It might be—" And he, too, stopped at the actual voicing of the wild surmise. He shook his head sharply as if to rid it of intruding, unwelcome thoughts.

"Forget that!" he told McGuire, and repeated it in a less commanding tone. "Forget it, Mac: we've got to render a report to sane men, you and I. What we know will be hard enough for them to believe without any wild guesses.

"That new craft is real. It has got it all over us for size and speed and potential offensive action. Who made it? Who mans it? Red Russia? Japan? That's what the brass hats will be wondering; that's what they will want to find out.

"Not a word!" he repeated to the radio man. "You will keep mum on this."

He took McGuire with him as he left to seek out his colonel. But it was a disturbed and shaken man, instead of the cool, methodical Captain Blake of ordinary days, who went in search of his commanding officer. And he clung to McGuire for corroboration of his impossible story.

There was a group of officers to whom Blake made his full report. Colonel Boynton had heard but little when he halted his subordinate curtly and reached for a phone. And his words over that instrument brought a quick conference of officers and a quiet man whom McGuire did not recognize. The "brass hats," as Blake had foreseen, were avid for details.

The pilot of the incoming plane was there, too, and the radio man. Their stories were told in a disconcerting silence, broken only by some officer's abrupt and skeptical question on one point and another.

"Now, for heaven's sake, shut up about Venus," McGuire had been told. But he did not need Captain Blake's warning to hold himself strictly to what he had seen and let the others draw their own conclusions.

Lieutenant McGuire was the last one to speak. There was silence in the office of Colonel Boynton as he finished, a silence that almost echoed from the grim walls. And the faces of the men who gathered there were carefully masked from any expression that might betray their thoughts.

It was the quiet man in civilian attire who spoke first. He sat beside another whose insignia proclaimed him of general's rank, but he addressed himself to Colonel Boynton.

"I am very glad," he said quietly, "very glad. Colonel, that my unofficial visit came at just this time. I should like to ask some few questions."

Colonel Boynton shifted the responsibility with a gesture almost of relief. "It is in your hands. Mr. Secretary," he said. "You and General Clinton have dropped in opportunely. There is something here that will tax all our minds."

The man in civilian clothes nodded assent. He turned to Captain Blake.

"Captain," he said, "you saw this at first hand. You have told us what you saw. I should like greatly to know what you think. Will you give us your opinion, your impressions?"

The captain arose smartly, but his words came with less ease.

"My opinion," he stated, "will be of little value, but it is based upon these facts. I have seen to-night, sir, a new type of aircraft, with speed, climb and ceiling beyond anything we are capable of. I can only regard it as a menace. It may or may not have been armed, but it had the size to permit the armament of a cruiser; it had power to carry that weight. It hung stationary in the air, so it is independent of wing-lift, yet it turned and shot upward like a feather in a gale. That spells maneuverability.

"That combination, sir, can mean only that we are out-flown, out-maneuvered and out-fought in the air. It means that the planes in our hangars are obsolete, our armament so much old iron.

"The menace is potential at present. Whether it is an actual threat or not is another matter. Who mans that ship—what country's insignia she carries—is something on which I can have no opinion. The power is there: who wields it I wish we knew."

The questioner nodded at the conclusion of Blake's words, and he exchanged quiet, grave glances with the general beside him. Then—

"I think we all would wish to know that, Captain Blake," he observed. And to the colonel: "You may be able to answer that soon. It would be my idea that this craft should be—ah—drawn out, if we can do it. We would not attack it, of course, until its mission is proved definitely unfriendly, but you will resist any offensive from them.

"And now," he added, "let us thank these officers for their able reports and excuse them. We have much to discuss...."

Captain Blake took McGuire's arm as they went out into the night. And he drew him away where they walked for silent minutes by themselves. The eyes of Lieutenant McGuire roamed upward to the scudding clouds and the glimpse of far, lonely stars; he stumbled occasionally as he walked. But for Captain Blake there was thought only of matters nearby.

"The old fox!" he exclaimed. "Didn't he 'sic us on' neatly? If we mix it with that stranger there will be no censure from the Secretary of War."

"I assumed that was who it was," said McGuire. "Well, they have something to think about, that bunch; something to study over.... Perhaps more than they know.

"And that's their job," he concluded after a silence. "I'm going to bed; but I would like a leave of absence to-morrow if that's O. K."

"Sure," said Captain Blake, "though I should think you would like to stick around. Perhaps we will see something. What's on your mind, Mac?"

"A little drive to the top of Mount Lawson," said Lieutenant McGuire. "I want to talk to a bird named Sykes."

CHAPTER II

Lieutenant McGuire, U. S. A., was not given as a usual thing to vain conjectures, nor did his imagination carry him beyond the practical boundaries of accepted facts. Yet his mind, as he drove for hours through the orange-scented hills of California, reverted time and again to one persistent thought. And it was with him still, even when he was consciously concentrating on the hairpin turns of Mount Lawson's narrow road.

There was a picture there, printed indelibly in his mind—a picture of a monstrous craft, a liner of the air, that swung its glowing lights in a swift arc and, like a projectile from some huge gun, shot up and up and still up until it vanished in a jet-black sky. Its altitude when it passed from sight he could not even guess, but the sense of ever-increasing speed, of power that mocked at gravitation's puny force, had struck deep into his mind. And McGuire saw plainly this mystery ship going on and on far into the empty night where man had never been.

No lagging in that swift flight that he had seen; an acceleration that threw the ship faster and yet faster, regardless of the thin air and the lessened buoyancy in an ocean of atmosphere that held man-made machines so close to Earth. That constant acceleration, hour after hour, day after day—the speed would be almost unlimited; inconceivable!

He stopped his car where the mountain road held straight for a hundred feet, and he looked out over the coastal plain spread like a toy world far below.

"Now, how about it?" he asked himself. "Blake thinks I am making a fool of myself. Perhaps I am. I wonder. It's a long time since I fell for any fairy stories. But this thing has got me. A sort of hunch, I guess."

The sun was shining now from a vault of clear blue. It was lighting a world of reality, of houses where people lived their commonplace lives, tiny houses squared off in blocks a mile below. There was smoke here and there from factories; it spread in a haze, and it meant boilers and engines and sound practical machinery of a practical world to the watching man.

What had all this to do with Venus? he asked himself. This was the world he knew. It was real; space was impenetrable; there were no men or beings of any sort that could travel through space. Blake was right: he was on a fool's errand. They couldn't tell him anything up here at the observatory; they would laugh at him as he deserved....

Wondering vaguely if there was a place to turn around, he looked ahead and then up; his eyes passed from the gash of roadway on the mountainside to the deep blue beyond. And within the man some driving, insistent, mental force etched strongly before his eyes that picture and its problem unanswered. There was the ship—he saw it in memory—and it went up and still up; and he knew as surely as if he had guided the craft that the meteor-like flight could be endless.

Lieutenant McGuire could not reason it out—such power was beyond his imagining—but suddenly he dared to believe, and he knew it was true.

"Earthbound!" he said in contempt of his own human kind, and he looked again at the map spread below. "Ants! Mites! That's what we are—swarming across the surface of the globe. And we think we're so damn clever if we lift ourselves up a few miles from the surface!

"Guess I'll see Sykes," he muttered aloud. "He and his kind at least dare to look out into space; take their eyes off the world; be impractical!"

He swung the car slowly around the curve ahead, eased noiselessly into second gear and went on with the climb.

There were domed observatories where he stopped: rounded structures that gleamed silvery in the air; and offices, laboratories: it was a place of busy men. And Professor Sykes, he found, was busy. But he spared a few minutes to answer courteously the questions of this slim young fellow in the khaki uniform of the air service.

"What can I do for you?" asked Professor Sykes.

"No dreamer, this man," thought McGuire as he looked at the short, stocky figure of the scientist. Clear eyes glanced sharply from under shaggy brows; there were papers in his hand scrawled over with strange mathematical symbols.

"You can answer some fool questions," said Lieutenant McGuire abruptly, "if you don't mind."

The scientist smiled broadly. "We're used to that," he told the young officer; "you can't think of any worse ones than those we have heard. Have a chair."

McGuire drew a clipping from his pocket—it was the newspaper account he had read—and he handed it to Professor Sykes.

"I came to see you about this," he began.

The lips of Professor Sykes lost their genial curve; they straightened to a hard line. "Nothing for publication," he said curtly. "As usual they enlarged upon the report and made assumptions and inferences not warranted by facts."

"But you did see that flash?"

"By visual observation I saw a bright area formed on the terminator—yes! We have no photographic corroboration."

"I am wondering what it meant."

"That is your privilege—and mine," said the scientist coldly.

"But it said there," McGuire persisted, "that it might have been a signal of some sort."

"*I* did not say so: that is an inference only. I have told you, Lieutenant"—he glanced at the card in his hand—"—Lieutenant McGuire—all that I know. We deal in facts up here, and we leave the brilliant theorizing to the journalists."

The young officer felt distinctly disconcerted. He did not know exactly what he had expected from this man—what corroboration of his wild surmises—but he was getting nowhere, he admitted. And he resented the cold aloofness of the scientist before him.

"I am not trying to pin you down on anything," he said, and his tone carried a hint of the nervous strain that had been his. "I am trying to learn something."

"Just what?" the other inquired.

"Could that flash have been a signal?"

"You may think so if you wish: I have told you all that I know. And now," he added, and rose from his chair, "I must ask to be excused; I have work to do."

McGuire came slowly to his feet. He had learned nothing; perhaps there was nothing to be learned. A fool's errand! Blake was right. But the inner urge for some definite knowledge drove him on. His eyes were serious and his face drawn to a scowl of earnestness as he turned once more to the waiting man.

"Professor Sykes," he demanded, "just one more question. Could that have been the flash of a—a rocket? Like the proposed experiments in Germany. Could it have meant in any way the launching of a projectile—a ship—to travel Earthward through space?"

Professor Sykes knew what it was to be harassed by the curious mob, to avoid traps set by ingenious reporters, but he knew, too, when he was meeting with honest bewilderment and a longing for knowledge. His fists were placed firmly on the hips of his stocky figure as he stood looking at the persistent questioner, and his eyes passed from the intent face to the snug khaki coat and the spread wings that proclaimed the wearer's work. A ship out of space—a projectile—this young man had said.

"Lieutenant," he suggested quietly—and again the smile had returned to his lips as he spoke—"sit down. I'm not as busy as I pretend to be. Now tell me: what in the devil have you got in your mind?"

And McGuire told him. "Like some of your dope," he said, "this is not for publication. But I have not been instructed to hush it up, and I know you will keep it to yourself."

He told the clear-eyed, listening man of the previous night's events. Of the radio's weird call and the mystery ship.

"Hallucination," suggested the scientist. "You saw the stars very clearly, and they suggested a ship."

"Tell that to Jim Burgess," said McGuire: "he was the pilot of that plane." And the scientist nodded as if the answer were what he expected.

He asked again about the ship's flight. And he, too, bore down heavily upon the matter of acceleration in the thin upper air. He rose to lay a friendly hand on McGuire's shoulder.

"We can't know what it means," he said, "but we can form our own theories, you and I—and anything is possible.

"It is getting late," he added, "and you have had a long drive. Come over and eat; spend the night here. Perhaps you would like to have a look at our equipment—see Venus for yourself. I will be observing her through the sixty-inch refractor to-night. Would you care to?"

"Would I?" McGuire demanded with enthusiasm. "Say, that will be great!"

The sun was dropping toward the horizon when the two men again came out into the cool mountain air.

"Just time for a quick look around," suggested Professor Sykes, "if you are interested."

He took the lieutenant first to an enormous dome that bulged high above the ground, and admitted him to the dark interior. They climbed a stairway and came out into a room that held a skeleton frame of steel. "This is the big boy," said Professor Sykes, "the one hundred-inch reflector."

There were other workers there, one a man standing upon a raised platform beside the steel frame, who arranged big holders for photographic plates. The slotted ceiling opened as McGuire watched, and the whole structure swung slowly around. It was still, and the towering steel frame began to swing noiselessly when a man at a desk touched various controls. McGuire looked about him in bewilderment.

"Quite a shop," he admitted; "but where is the telescope?"

Professor Sykes pointed to the towering latticework of steel. "Right there," he said. "Like everyone else, you were expecting to see a big tube."

He explained in simple words the operation of the great instrument that brought in light rays from sources millions of light years away. He pointed out where the big mirror was placed—the one hundred-inch reflector—and he traced for the wondering man the pathway of light that finally converged upon a sensitized plate to catch and record what no eye had ever seen.

He checked the younger man's flow of questions and turned him back toward the stairs. "We will leave them to their work," he said; "they will be gathering light that has been traveling millions of years on its ways. But you and I have something a great deal nearer to study."

Another building held the big refractor, and it was a matter of only a few seconds and some cryptic instructions from Sykes until the eye-piece showed the image of the brilliant planet.

"The moon!" McGuire exclaimed in disappointed tones when the professor motioned him to see for himself. His eyes saw a familiar half-circle of light.

"Venus," the professor informed him. "It has phases like the moon. The planet is approaching; the sun's light strikes it from the side." But McGuire hardly heard. He was gazing with all his faculties centered upon that distant world, so near to him now.

"Venus," he whispered half aloud. Then to the professor: "It's all hazy. There are no markings—"

"Clouds," said the other. "The goddess is veiled; Venus is blanketed in clouds. What lies underneath we may never know, but we do know that of all the planets this is most like the earth; most probably is an inhabited world. Its size, its density, your weight if you were there—and the temperature under the sun's rays about double that of ours. Still, the cloud envelope would shield it."

McGuire was fascinated, and his thoughts raced wildly in speculation of what might be transpiring before his eyes. People, living in that tropical world; living and going through their daily routine under that cloud-filled sky where the sun was never seen. The margin of light that made the clear shape of a half-moon marked their daylight and dark; there was one small dot of light forming just beyond that margin. It penetrated the dark side. And it grew, as he watched, to a bright patch.

"What is that?" he inquired abstractedly—his thoughts were still filled with those beings of his imagination. "There is a light that extends into the dark part. It is spreading—"

He found himself thrust roughly aside as Professor Sykes applied a more understanding eye to the instrument.

The professor whirled abruptly to his assistant. "Phone Professor Giles," he said sharply; "he is working on the reflector. Tell him to get a photograph of Venus at once; the cloud envelope is broken." He returned hurriedly to his observations. One hand sketched on a waiting pad.

"Markings!" he said exultantly. "If it would only hold!... There, it is closing ... gone...."

His hand was quiet now upon the paper, but where he had marked was a crude sketch of what might have been an island. It was "L" shaped; sharply bent.

"Whew!" breathed Professor Sykes and looked up for a moment. "Now that was interesting."

"You saw through?" asked McGuire eagerly. "Glimpsed the surface?—an island?"

The scientist's face relaxed. "Don't jump to conclusions," he told the aviator: "we are not ready to make a geography of Venus quite yet. But we shall know that mark if we ever see it again. I hardly think they had time to get a picture.

"And now there is only a matter of three hours for observation: I must watch every minute. Stay here if you wish. But," he added, "don't let your imagination run wild. Some eruption, perhaps, this we have seen—an ignition of gasses in the upper air—who knows? But don't connect this with your mysterious ship. If the ship is a menace, if it means war, that is your field of action, not mine. And you will be fighting with someone on Earth. It must be that some country has gained a big lead in aeronautics. Now I must get to work."

"I'll not wait," said McGuire. "I will start for the field; get there by daylight, if I can find my way down that road in the dark."

"Thanks a lot." He paused a moment before concluding slowly: "And in spite of what you say, Professor, I believe that we will have something to get together on again in this matter."

The scientist, he saw, had turned again to his instrument. McGuire picked his way carefully along the narrow path that led where he had parked his car. "Good scout, this Sykes!" he was thinking, and he stopped to look overhead in the quick-gathering dark at that laboratory of the heavens, where Sykes and his kind delved and probed, measured and weighed, and gathered painstakingly the messages from suns beyond counting, from universe out there in space that added their bit of enlightenment to the great story of the mystery of creation.

He was humbly aware of his own deep ignorance as he backed his car, slipped it into second, and began the long drive down the tortuous grade. He would have liked to talk more with Sykes. But he had no thought as he wound round the curves how soon that wish was to be gratified.

Part way down the mountainside he again checked his car where he had stopped on the upward climb and reasoned with himself about his errand. Once more he looked out over the level ground below, a vast glowing expanse of electric lights now, that stretched to the ocean beyond. He was suddenly unthrilled by this man-made illumination, and he got out of his car to stare again at the blackness above and its myriad of stars that gathered and multiplied as he watched.

One brighter than the rest winked suddenly out. There was a constellation of twinkling lights that clustered nearby, and they too vanished. The eyes of the watcher strained themselves to see more clearly a dim-lit outline. There were no lights: it was a black shape, lost in the blackness of the mountain sky, that was blocking out the stars. But it was a shape, and from near the horizon the pale gleams of the rising moon picked it out in softest of outline; a vague ghost of a curve that reflected a silvery contour to the watching eyes below.

There had been a wider space in the road that McGuire had passed; he backed carefully till he could swing his car and turn it to head once more at desperate speed toward the mountain top. And it was less than an hour since he had left when he was racing back along the narrow footpath to slam open the door where Professor Sykes looked up in amazement at his abrupt return.

The aviator's voice was hoarse with excitement as he shouted: "It's here—the ship! It's here! Where's your phone?—I must call the field! It's right overhead—descending slowly—no lights, but I saw it—I saw it!"

He was working with trembling fingers at the phone where Sykes had pointed. "Long distance!" he shouted. He gave a number to the operator. "Make it quick," he implored. "Quick!"

CHAPTER III

Back at Maricopa Flying Field the daily routine had been disturbed. There were conferences of officers, instructions from Colonel Boynton, and a curiosity-provoking lack of explanations. Only with Captain Blake did the colonel indulge in any discussion.

"We'll keep this under our hats," he said, "and out of the newspapers as long as we can. You can imagine what the yellow journals would do with a scarehead like that. Why, they would have us all wiped off the map and the country devastated by imaginary fleets in the first three paragraphs."

Blake regarded his superior gravely. "I feel somewhat the same way, myself. Colonel," he admitted. "When I think what this can mean—some other country so far ahead of us in air force that we are back in the dark ages—well, it doesn't look any too good to me if they mean trouble."

"We will meet it when it comes," said Colonel Boynton. "But, between ourselves, I am in the same state of mind.

"The whole occurrence is so damn mysterious. Washington hasn't a whisper of information of any such construction; the Secretary admitted that last night. It's a surprise, a complete surprise, to everyone.

"But, Blake, you get that new ship ready as quickly as you can. Prepare for an altitude test the same as we planned, but get into the air the first minute possible. She ought to show a better ceiling than anything we have here, and you may have to fly high to say 'Good morning' to that liner you saw. Put all the mechanics on it that can work to advantage. I think they have it pretty well along now."

"Engine's tested and installed, sir," was Blake's instant report. "I think I can take it up this afternoon."

He left immediately to hurry to the hangar where a new plane stood glistening in pristine freshness, and where hurrying mechanics grumbled under their breaths at the sudden rush for a ship that was expected to take the air a week later.

An altitude test under full load! Well, what of it? they demanded one of another; wouldn't another day do as well as this one? And they worked as they growled, worked with swift sureness and skill, and the final instruments took their place in the ship that she might roll from the hangar complete under that day's sun.

Her supercharger was tested—the adjunct to a powerful engine that would feed the hungry cylinders with heavy air up in the heights where the air is thin; there were oxygen flasks to keep life in the pilot in the same thin air. And the hot southern sun made ludicrous that afternoon the bulky, heavily-wrapped figure of Captain Blake as he sat at the controls and listened approvingly to the roaring engine.

He waved good-by and smiled understandingly as he met the eyes of Colonel Boynton; then pulled on his helmet, settled himself in his seat and took off in a thunderous blast of sound to begin his long ascent.

He had long since cracked open the valve of his oxygen flask when the climb was ended, and his goggles were frosted in the arctic cold so that it was only with difficulty he could read his instrument board.

"That's the top," he thought in that mind so light and so curiously not his own. He throttled the engine and went into a long spiral that was to end within a rod of where he had started on the brown sun-baked field. The last rays of the sun were slanting over distant mountains as he climbed stiffly from the machine.

"Better than fifty thousand," exulted Colonel Boynton. "Of course your barograph will have to be calibrated and verified, but it looks like a record, Blake—and you had a full load.

"Ready to go up and give merry hell to that other ship if she shows up?" he asked. But Captain Blake shook a dubious head.

"Fifty thousand is just a start for that bird," he said. "You didn't see them shoot out of sight, Colonel. Lord knows when they quit *their* climb—or where."

"Well, we'll just have a squadron ready in any event," the colonel assured him. "We will make him show his stuff or take a beating—if that is what he wants."

They were in the colonel's office. "You had better go and get warmed up," he told the flyer: "then come back here for instructions." But Blake was more anxious for information than for other comforts.

"I'm all right," he said: "just tired a bit. Let me stretch out here, Colonel, and give me the dope on what you expect of our visitor and what we will do."

He settled back comfortably in a big chair. The office was warm, and Blake knew now he had been doing a day's work.

"We will just take it as it comes," Colonel Boynton explained. "I can't for the life of me figure why the craft was spying around here. What are they looking for? We haven't any big secrets the whole world doesn't know.

"Of course he may not return. But if he does I want you to go up and give him the once over. I can trust you to note every significant detail.

"You saw no wings. If it is a dirigible, let's know something of their power and how they can throw themselves up into the air the way you described. Watch for anything that may serve to identify it and its probable place of manufacture—any peculiarity of marking or design or construction that may give us a lead. Then return and report."

Blake nodded his understanding of what was wanted, but his mind was on further contingencies: he wanted definite instructions.

"And," he asked; "if they attack—what then? Is their fire to be returned?"

"If they make one single false move," said Colonel Boynton savagely, "give them everything you've got. And the 91st Squadron will be off the ground to support you at the first sign of trouble. We don't want to start anything, nor appear to do so. But, by the gods, Blake, this fellow means trouble eventually as sure as you're a flyer, and we won't wait for him to ask for it twice."

They sat in silence, while the field outside became shrouded in night. And they speculated, as best they could from the few facts they had, as to what this might mean to the world, to their country, to themselves. It was an hour before Blake was aware of the fact that he was hungry.

He rose to leave, but paused while Colonel Boynton answered the phone. The first startled exclamation held him rigid while he tried to piece together the officer's curt responses and guess at what was being told.

"Colonel Boynton speaking.... McGuire?... Yes, Lieutenant.... Over Mount Lawson?... Yes—yes, the same ship, I've no doubt."

His voice was even and cool in contrast to the excited tones that carried faintly to Blake standing by.

"Quite right!" he said shortly. "You will remain where you are: act as observer: hold this line open and keep me informed. Captain Blake will leave immediately for observation. A squadron will follow. Let me know promptly what you see."

He turned abruptly to the waiting man.

"It is back!" he said. "We're in luck! Over the observatories at Mount Lawson; descending, so Lieutenant McGuire says. Take the same ship you had up to-day. Look them over—get up close—good luck!" He turned again to the phone.

There were planes rolling from their hangars before Blake could reach his own ship. Their engines were thundering: men were rushing across the field, pulling on leather helmets and coats as they ran—all this while he warmed up his engine.

A mechanic thrust in a package of sandwiches and a thermos of coffee while he waited. And Captain Blake grinned cheerfully and gulped the last of his food as he waved to the mechanics to pull out the wheel blocks. He opened the throttle and shot out into the dark.

He climbed and circled the field, saw the waving motion of lights in red and green that marked the take-off of the planes of the 91st, and he straightened out on a course that in less than two hours would bring him over the heights of Mount Lawson and the mystery that awaited him there. And he fingered the trigger grip that was part of the stick and nodded within his dark cockpit at the rattle of a machine gun that merged its staccato notes with the engine's roar.

But he felt, as he thought of that monster shape, as some primordial man might have felt, setting forth with a stone in his hand to wage war on a saurian beast.

CHAPTER IV

If Colonel Boynton could have stood with one of his lieutenants and Professor Sykes on a mountain top, he would have found, perhaps, the answer to his question. He had wondered in a puzzled fashion why the great ship had shown its mysterious presence over the flying field. He had questioned whether it was indeed the field that had been the object of their attention or whether in the cloudy murk they had merely wandered past. Could he have seen with the eyes of Lieutenant McGuire the descent of the great shape over Mount Lawson, he would have known beyond doubt that here was the magnet that drew the eyes of whatever crew was manning the big craft.

It was dark where the two men stood. Others had come running at their call, but their forms, too, were lost in the shadows of the towering pines. The light from an open door struck across an open space beyond which McGuire and Professor Sykes stood alone, stood silent and spellbound, their heads craned back at a neck-wrenching angle. They were oblivious to all discomforts; their eyes and their whole minds were on the unbelievable thing in the sky.

Beyond the fact that no lights were showing along the hull, there was no effort at concealment. The moon was up now to illumine the scene, and it showed plainly the gleaming cylinder with its long body and blunt, shining ends, dropping, slowly, inexorably down.

"Like a dirigible," said McGuire huskily. "But the size, man—the size! And its shape is not right; it isn't streamlined correctly; the air—" He stopped his half-unconscious analysis abruptly. "The air!" What had this craft to do with the air? A thin layer of gas that hung close to the earth—the skin on an apple! And beyond—space! There was the ethereal ocean in which this great shape swam!

The reality of the big ship, the very substance of it, made the space ship idea the harder to grasp. Lieutenant McGuire found that it was easier to see an imaginary craft taking off into space than to conceive of this monstrous shape, many hundreds of tons in weight, being thrown through vast emptiness. Yet he knew; he knew!

And his mind was a chaos of grim threats and forebodings as he looked at the unbelievable reality and tried to picture what manner of men were watching, peering, from those rows of ports.

At last it was motionless. It hung soundless and silent except for a soft roar, a scant thousand feet in the air. And its huge bulk was dwarfing the giant pines, the rounded buildings; it threw the men's familiar surroundings into a new and smaller scale.

He had many times flown over these mountains, and Lieutenant McGuire had seen the silvery domes of the observatories shining among the trees. Like fortresses for aerial defense, he had thought, and the memory returned to him now. What did these new-comers think of them? Had they, too, found them suggestive of forts on the frontier of a world, defenses against invasion from out there? Or did they know them for what they were? Did they wish only to learn the extent of our knowledge, our culture? Were they friendly, perhaps?—half-timid and fearful of what they might find?

A star moved in the sky, a pin-point of light that was plain in its message to the aviator. It was Blake, flying high, volplaning to make contact and learn from the air what this stranger might mean. The light of his plane slanted down in an easy descent; the flyer was gliding in on a long aerial toboggan slide. His motor was throttled; there was only the whistle of torn air on the monoplane's wings. McGuire was with the captain in his mind, and like him he was waiting for whatever the stranger might do.

Other lights were clustered where the one plane had been. The men of the 91st had their orders, and the fingers of the watching, silent man gripped an imaginary stick while he wished with his whole heart that he was up in the air. To be with Blake or the others! His thoughts whipped back to the mysterious stranger: the great shape was in motion: it rose sharply a thousand feet in the air.

The approaching plane showed clear in the moon's light. It swung and banked, and the vibrant song of its engine came down to the men as Blake swept in a great circle about the big ship. He was looking it over, but he began his inspection at a distance, and the orbit of his plane made a tightening spiral as he edged for a closer look. He was still swinging in the monotonous round when the ship made its first forward move.

It leaped in the air: it swept faster and faster. And it was moving with terrific speed as it crashed silently through the path of the tiny plane. And Blake, as he leaned forward on the stick to throw his plane downward in a power dive, could have had a vision, not of a ship of the air, but only of a shining projectile as the great monster shrieked overhead.

McGuire trembled for the safety of those wings as he saw Blake pull his little ship out of the dive and shoot upward to a straight climb.

But—"That's dodging them!" he exulted: "that's flying! I wonder, did they mean to wipe him out or were they only scared off?"

His question was answered as, out of the night, a whistling shriek proclaimed the passage of the meteor ship that drove unmistakably at the lone plane. And again the pilot with superb skill waited until the last moment and threw himself out of the path of the oncoming mass, though his own plane was tossed and whirled like an autumn leaf in the vortex that the enemy created. Not a second was lost as Blake opened his throttle and forced his plane into a steep climb.

"Atta-boy!" said McGuire, as if words could span across to the man in the plane. "Altitude, Blake—get altitude!"

The meteor had turned in a tremendous circle; so swift its motion that it made an actual line of light as the moon marked its course. And the curved line straightened abruptly to a flashing mark that shot straight toward the struggling plane.

This time another sound came down to the listening ears of the two men. The plane tore head on to meet the onslaught, to swing at the last instant in a frantic leap that ended as before in the maelstrom of air back of the ship. But the muffled roar was changed, punctured with a machine-gun's familiar rattle, and the stabbing flashes from Blake's ship before he threw it out of the other's path were a song of joy to the tense nerves of the men down below.

This deadly rush could only be construed as an attack, and Blake was fighting back. The very speed of the great projectile must hold it to its course; the faster it went the more difficult to swerve it from a line. This and much more was flashing sharply in McGuire's mind. But—Blake!—alone against this huge antagonist!... It was coming back. Another rush like a star through space....

And McGuire shouted aloud in a frenzy of emotion as a cluster of lights came falling from on high. No lone machine gun now that tore the air with this clattering bedlam of shots: the planes of the 91st Squadron were diving from the heights. They came on a steep slant that seemed marking them for crashing death against the huge cylinder flashing past. And their stabbing needles of machine-gun fire made a drumming tattoo, till the planes, with the swiftness of hawks, swept aside, formed to groups, tore on down toward the ground and then curved in great circles of speed to climb back to the theater of action.

Lieutenant McGuire was rigid and quivering. He should go to the phone and report to the colonel, but the thought left him as quickly as it came. He was frozen in place, and his mind could hold only the scene that was being pictured before him.

The enemy ship had described its swift curve, and the planes of the defenders were climbing desperately for advantage. So slowly they moved as compared with the swiftness of the other!

But the great ship was slowing; it came on, but its wild speed was checked. The light of the full moon showed plainly now what McGuire had seen but dimly before—a great metal beak on the ship, pointed and shining, a ram whose touch must bring annihilation to anything it struck.

The squadron of planes made a group in the sky, and Blake's monoplane, too, was with them. The huge enemy was approaching slowly: was it damaged? McGuire hardly dared hope ... yet that raking fire might well have been deadly: it might be that some bullets had torn and penetrated to the vitals of this ship's machinery and damaged some part.

It came back slowly, ominously, toward the circling planes. Then, throwing itself through the air, it leaped not directly toward them but off to one side.

Like a stone on the end of a cord it swung with inconceivable speed in a circle that enclosed the group of planes. Again and again it whipped around them, while the planes, by comparison, were motionless. Its orbit was flat with the ground: then tilting, more yet, it made a last circle that stood like a hoop in the air. And behind it as it circled it left a faint trace of vapor. Nebulous!—milky in the moonlight!—but the ship had built a sphere, a great globe of the gas, and within it, like rats in a cage, the planes of the 91st Squadron were darting and whirling.

"Gas!" groaned the watching man: "gas! What is it? Why don't they break through?"

The thin clouds of vapor were mingling now and expanding: they blossomed and mushroomed, and the light of the moon came in pale iridescence from their billowing folds.

"Break through!" McGuire had prayed—and he stood in voiceless horror as he saw the attempt.

The mist was touching here and there a plane: they were engulfed, yet he could see them plainly. And he saw with staring, fear-filled eyes the clumsy tumbling and fluttering of unguided wings as the great eagles of the 91st fell roaring to earth with no conscious minds guiding their flight.

The valleys were deep about the mountain, and their shadowed blackness opened to receive the maimed, stricken things that came fluttering or swooping wildly to that last embrace, where, in the concealing shadows, the deeper shadows of death awaited....

There was a room where a telephone waited: McGuire sensed this but dumbly, and the way to that room was long to his stumbling feet. He was blinded: his mind would not function: he saw only those fluttering things, and the moonlight on their wings, and the shadows that took them so softly at the last.

One plane whistled close overhead. McGuire stopped where he stood to follow it with unbelieving eyes. That one man had lived, escaped the net—it was inconceivable! The plane returned: it was flying low, and it swerved erratically as it flew. It was a monoplane: a new ship.

Its motor was silenced: it stalled as he watched, to pancake and crash where the towering pines made a cradle of great branches to cushion its fall.

No thought now of the colonel waiting impatiently for a report; even the enemy, there in the sky was forgotten. It was Blake in that ship, and he was alive—or had been—for he had cut his motor. McGuire screamed out for Professor Sykes, and there were others, too, who came running at his call. He tore recklessly through the scrub and undergrowth and gained at last the place where wreckage hung dangling from the trees. The fuselage of a plane, scarred and broken, was still held in the strong limbs.

Captain Blake was in the cockpit, half hanging from the side. He was motionless, quiet, and his face shone white and ghastly as they released him and drew him out. But one hand still clung with a grip like death itself to a hose that led from an oxygen tank. McGuire stared in wonder and slowly gathering comprehension.

"He was fixed for an altitude test," he said dazedly; "this ship was to be used, and he was to find her ceiling. He saw what the others were getting, and he flew himself through on a jet of pure oxygen—" He stopped in utter admiration of the quickness of thought that could outwit death in an instant like that.

They carried the limp body to the light. "No bones broken so far as I can see," said the voice of Professor Sykes. "Leave him here in the air. He must have got a whiff of their devilish mist in spite of his oxygen; he was flying mighty awkwardly when he came in here."

But he was alive!—and Lieutenant McGuire hastened with all speed now to the room where a telephone was ringing wildly and a colonel of the air force must be told of the annihilation of a crack squadron and of a threat that menaced all the world.

In that far room there were others waiting where Colonel Boynton sat with receiver to his ear. A general's uniform was gleaming in the light to make more sober by contrast the civilian clothing of that quiet, clear-eyed man who held the portfolio of the Secretary of War.

They stared silently at Colonel Boynton, and they saw the blood recede from his face, while his cool voice went on unmoved with its replies.

"... I understand," he said; "a washout, complete except for Captain Blake; his oxygen saved him.... It attacked with gas, you say?... And why did not our own planes escape?... Its speed!—yes, we'll have to imagine it, but it is unbelievable. One moment—" He turned to those who waited for his report.

"The squadron," he said with forced quiet, though his lips twitched in a bloodless line, "—the 91st—is destroyed. The enemy put them down with one blow; enveloped them with gas." He recounted the essence of McGuire's report, then turned once more to the phone.

"Hello, Lieutenant—the enemy ship—where is it now?"

He listened—listened—to a silent receiver: silent save for the sound of a shot—a crashing fall—a loud, panting breath. He heard the breathing close to the distant instrument; it ended in a choking gasp; the instrument was silent in his ear....

He signalled violently for the operator: ordered the ringing of any and all phones about the observatory, and listened in vain for a sound or syllable in reply.

"A plane," he told an orderly, "at once! Phone the commercial flying field near the base of Mount Lawson. Have them hold a car ready for me: I shall land there!"

CHAPTER V

To Captain Blake alone, of all those persons on the summit of Mount Lawson, it was given to see and to know and be able to relate what transpired there and in the air above. For Blake, although he appeared like one dead, was never unconscious throughout his experience.

Driving head on toward the ship, he had emptied his drum of cartridges before he threw his plane over and down in a dive that escaped the onrush of the great craft by a scant margin, and that carried him down in company with the men and machines of the squadron that dived from above.

He turned as they turned and climbed as they climbed for the advantage that altitude might give. And he climbed faster: his ship outdistanced them in that tearing, scrambling rush for the heights. The squadron was spiraling upward in close formation with his plane above them when the enemy struck.

He saw that great shape swing around them, terrible in its silent swiftness, and, like the others, he failed to realize at first the net she was weaving. So thin was the gas and so rapid the circling of the enemy craft, they were captured and cut off inside of the gaseous sphere before the purpose of the maneuver was seen or understood.

He saw the first faint vapor form above him; swung over for a steep bank that carried him around the inside of the great cage of gas and that showed him the spiraling planes as the first wisps of vapor swept past them.

He held that bank with his swift machine, while below him a squadron of close-formed fighting craft dissolved before his eyes into unguided units. The formations melted: wings touched and locked; the planes fell dizzily or shot off in wild, ungoverned, swerving flight. The air was misty about him; it was fragrant in his nostrils; the world was swimming....

It was gas, he knew, and with the light-headedness that was upon him, so curiously like that of excessive altitudes, he reached unconsciously for the oxygen supply. The blast of pure gas in his face revived him for an instant, and in that instant of clear thinking his plan was formed. He threw his weight on stick and rudder, corrected the skid his ship was taking, and, with one hand holding the tube of life-giving oxygen before his face, he drove straight down in a dive toward the earth.

There were great weights fastened to his arm, it seemed, when he tried to bring the ship from her fearful dive. He moved only with greatest effort, and it was force of will alone that compelled his hands to do their work. His brain, as he saw the gleaming roundness of observatory buildings beneath him, was as clear as ever in his life, but his muscles, his arms and legs, refused to work: even his head; he was slowly sinking beneath a load of utter fatigue.

The observatories were behind him; he must swing back; he could not last long, he knew; each slightest movement was intolerable effort.

Was this death? he wondered; but his mind was so clear! There were the buildings, the trees! How thickly they were massed beyond—

He brought every ounce of will power to bear ... the throttle!—and a slow glide in ... he was losing speed ... the stick—must—come—back! The crashing branches whipped about him, bending, crackling—and the world went dark....

There were stars above him when he awoke, and his back was wrenched and aching. He tried to move, to call, but found that the paralysing effect of the gas still held him fast. He was lying on the ground, he knew: a door was open in a building beyond, and the light in the room showed him men, a small group of them, standing silent while someone—yes, it was McGuire—shouted into a phone.

"... The squadron," he was saying. "... Lost! Every plane down and destroyed.... Blake is living but injured...." And then Blake remembered. And the tumbling, helpless planes came again before his eyes while he cursed silently at this freezing grip that would not let him cover his face with his hands to shut out the sight.

The figure of a man hurried past him, nor saw the body lying helpless in the cool dark. McGuire was still at the phone. And the enemy ship—?

His mind, filled with a welter of words as he tried to find phrases to compass his hate for that ship. And then, as if conjured out of nothing by his thoughts, the great craft itself came in view overhead in all its mighty bulk.

It settled down swiftly: it was riding on an even keel. And in silence and darkness it came from above. Blake tried to call out, but no sound could be formed by his paralyzed throat. Doors opened in silence, swinging down from the belly of the thing to show in the darkness square openings through which shot beams of brilliant yellow light.

There were cages that lowered—great platforms in slings—and the platforms came softly to rest on the ground. They were moving with life; living beings clustered upon them thick in the dark. Oh God! for an instant's release from the numbness that held his lips and throat to cry out one word!... The shapes were passing now in the shelter of darkness, going toward the room.... He could see McGuire's back turned toward the door.

Man-shapes, tall and thin, distorted humans, each swathed in bulging garments; horrible staring eyes of glass in the masks about their heads, and each hand ready with a shining weapon as they stood waiting for the men within to move.

McGuire must have seen them first, though his figure was half concealed from Blake where he was lying. But he saw the head turn; knew by the quick twist of the shoulders the man was reaching for a gun. One shot echoed in Blake's ears; one bulging figure spun and fell awkwardly to the ground; then the weapons in those clumsy hands hissed savagely while jets of vapor, half liquid and half gas, shot blindingly into the room. The faces dropped from his sight....

There had been the clamor of surprised and shouting men: there was silence now. And the awkward figures in the bloated casings that protected their bodies from the gas passed in safety to the room. Blake, bound in the invisible chains of enemy gas, struggled silently, futilely, to pit his will against this grip that held him. To lie there helpless, to see these men slaughtered! He saw one of the creatures push the body of his fallen comrade out of the way: it was cast aside with an indifferent foot.

They were coming back: Blake saw the form of McGuire in unmistakable khaki. He and another man were carried high on the shoulders of some of the invaders. They were going toward the platforms, the slings beneath the ship.... They passed close to Blake, and again he was unnoticed in the dark.

A clamor came from distant buildings, a babel of howls and shrieks, inhuman, unearthly. There were no phrases or syllables, but to Blake it was familiar ... somewhere he had heard it ... and then he remembered the radio and the weird wailing note that told of communication. These things were talking in the same discordant din.

They were gathering now on the platforms slung under the ship. A whistling note from somewhere within the great structure and the platforms went high in the air. They were loaded, he saw, with papers and books and instruments plundered from the observatories. Some made a second trip to take up the loot they had gathered. Then the black doorways closed; the huge bulk of the ship floated high above the trees; it took form, dwindled smaller and smaller, then vanished from sight in the star-studded sky.

Blake thought of their unconscious passenger—the slim figure of Lieutenant McGuire. Mac had been a close friend and a good one; his ready smile; his steady eyes that could tear a problem to pieces with their analytic scrutiny or gaze far into space to see those visions of a dreamer!

"Far into space." Blake repeated the words in his mind. And: "Good-by Mac," he said softly; "you've shipped for a long cruise, I'm thinking." He hardly realized he had spoken the words aloud.

Lying there in the cold night he felt his strength returning slowly. The pines sang their soothing, whispered message, and the faint night noises served but to intensify the silence of the mountain. It was some time before the grind of straining gears came faintly in the air to announce the coming of a car up the long grade. And still later he heard it come to a stop some distance beyond. There were footsteps, and voices calling: he heard the voice of Colonel Boynton. And he was able to call out in reply, even to move his head and turn it to see the approaching figures in the night.

Colonel Boynton knelt beside him. "Did they get you, old man?" he asked.

"Almost," Blake told him. "My oxygen—I was lucky. But the others—". He did not need to complete the sentence. The silent canyons among those wooded hills told plainly the story of the lost men.

"We will fight them with gas masks," said the colonel; "your experience has taught us the way."

"Gas-tight uniforms and our own supplies of oxygen," Blake supplemented. He told Boynton of the man-things he had seen come from the ship, of their baggy suits, their helmets.... And he had seen a small generator on the back of each helmet. He told him of the small, shining weapons and their powerful jets of gas. Deadly and unescapable at short range, he well knew.

"They got McGuire," Blake concluded; "carried him off a prisoner. Took another man, too."

For a moment Colonel Boynton's quiet tones lost their even steadiness. "We'll get them," he said savagely, and it was plain that it was the invaders that filled his mind; "we'll go after them, and we'll get them in spite of their damn gas, and we'll rip their big ship into ribbons—"

Captain Blake was able to raise a dissenting hand. "We will have to go where they are, Colonel, to do that."

Colonel Boynton stared at him. "Well?" he demanded. "Why not?"

"We can't go where *they* went," said Blake simply. "I laughed at McGuire; told him not to be a fool. But I was the fool—the blind one; we all were, Colonel. That thing came here out of space. It has gone back; it is far beyond our air. I saw it go up out of sight, and I know. Those creatures were men, if you like, but no men that we know—not those shrieking, wailing devils! And we're going to hear more from them, now that they've found their way here!"

CHAPTER VI

A score of bodies where men had died in strangling fumes in the observatories on Mount Lawson; one of the country's leading astronomical scientists vanished utterly; the buildings on the mountain top ransacked; papers and documents blowing in vagrant winds; tales of a monster ship in the air, incredibly huge, unbelievably swift—

There are matters that at times are not allowed to reach the press, but not happenings like these. And the papers of the United States blazed out with headlines to tell the world of this latest mystery.

Then came corroboration from the far corners of the world. The mystery ship had not visited one section only; it had made a survey of the whole civilized sphere, and the tales of those who had seen it were no longer laughed to scorn but went on the wires of the great press agencies to be given to the world. And with that the censorship imposed by the Department of War broke down, and the tragic story of the destruction of the 91st Air Squadron passed into written history. The wild tale of Captain Blake was on every tongue.

An invasion from space! The idea was difficult to accept. There were scoffers who tried to find something here for their easy wit. Why should we be attacked? What had that other world to gain? There was no answer ready, but the silent lips of the men who had fallen spoke eloquently of the truth. And the world, in wonder and consternation, was forced to believe.

Were there more to come? How meet them? Was this war—and with whom? What neighboring planet could reasonably be suspected. What had science to say?

The scientists! The scientists! The clamor of the world was beating at the doors of science and demanding explanations and answers. And science answered.

A conference was arranged in London; the best minds in the realms of astronomy and physics came together. They were the last to admit the truth that would not be denied, but admit it they must. And to some of the questions they found their answer.

It was not Mars, they said, though this in the popular mind was the source of the trouble. Not Mars, for that planet was far in the heavens. But Venus!—misnamed for the Goddess of Love. It was Venus, and she alone, who by any stretch of the imagination could be threatening Earth.

What did it mean? They had no answer. The ship was the only answer to that. Would there be more?—could we meet them?—defeat them? And again the wise men of the world refused to hazard a guess.

But they told what they knew; that Venus was past her eastern elongation, was approaching the earth. She of all the planets that swung around the sun came nearest to Earth—twenty-six million miles in another few weeks. Then whirling away she would pass to the western elongation in a month and a half and drive out into space. Venus circled the sun in a year of 225 days, and in 534 days she would again reach her eastern elongation with reference to the earth, and draw near us again.

They were reluctant to express themselves, these men who made nothing of weighing and analyzing stars a million of light years away, but *if* the popular conception was correct and *if* we could pass through the following weeks without further assault, we could count on a year and a half before the menace would again return. And in a year and a half—well, the physicists would be working—and we might be prepared.

Captain Blake had made his report, but this, it seemed, was not enough. He was ordered to come to Washington, and, with Colonel Boynton, he flew across the country to tell again his incredible story.

It was a notable gathering before which he appeared. All the branches of the service were represented; there were men in the uniform of admirals and generals; there were heads of Departments. And the Secretary of War was in charge.

He told his story, did Blake, before a battery of hostile eyes. This was not a gathering to be stampeded by wild scareheads, nor by popular clamor. They wanted facts, and they wanted them proved. But the gravity with which they regarded the investigation was shown by their invitation to the representatives of foreign powers to attend.

"I have told you all that happened," Blake concluded, "up to the coming of Colonel Boynton. May I reiterate one fact? I do not wonder at your questioning my state of mind and my ability to observe correctly. But I must insist, gentlemen, that while I got a shot of their gas and my muscles and my nervous system were paralyzed, my brain was entirely clear. I saw what I saw; those creatures were there; they entered the buildings; they carried off Lieutenant McGuire and another man.

"What they were or who they were I cannot say. I do not know that they were men, but their insane shrieking in that queer unintelligible talk is significant. And that means of communication corresponds with the radio reception of which you know.

"If you gentlemen know of any part of this earth that can produce such a people, if you know of any people or country in this world that can produce such a ship—then we can forget all our wild fancies. And we can prepare to submit to that country and that people as the masters of this earth. For I must tell you, gentlemen, with all the earnestness at my command, that until you have seen that ship in action, seen its incredible speed, its maneuverability, its lightning-like attack and its curtain of gas, you can have no conception of our helplessness. And the insignia that she carries is the flag of our conquerors."

Blake got an approving nod from the Secretary of War as he took his seat. That quiet man rose slowly from his chair to add his words. He spoke earnestly, impressively.

"Captain Blake has hit the nail squarely on the head," he stated. "We have here in this room a representative gathering from the whole world. If there is any one of you who can say that this mystery ship was built and manned by your people, let him speak, and we will send you at once a commission to acknowledge your power and negotiate for peace."

The great hall was silent, in a silence that held only uneasy rustlings as men glanced one at another in wondering dismay.

"The time has come," said the Secretary with solemn emphasis, "when all dissensions among our peoples must cease. Whatever there is or ever has been of discord between us fades into insignificance before this new threat. It is the world, now, against a power unknown; we can only face it as a united world.

"I shall recommend to the President of the United States that a commission be appointed, that it may co-operate with similar bodies from all lands. I ask you, gentlemen, to make like representations to your governments, to the end that we may meet this menace as one country and one man; meet it, God grant, successfully through a War Department of the World."

It was a brave gesture of the President of the United States; he dared the scorn and laughter of the world in standing behind his Secretary of War. The world is quick to turn and rend with ridicule a false prophet. And despite the unanswerable facts, the scope and power of the menace was not entirely believed. It was difficult for the conscious minds of men to conceive of the barriers of vast space as swept aside and the earth laid open to attack.

England was slow to respond to the invitation of the President: this matter required thought and grave deliberation in parliament. It might not be true: the thought, whether spoken or unexpressed, was clinging to their minds. And even if true—even if this lone ship had wandered in from space—there might be no further attack.

"Why," they asked, "should there be more unprovoked assaults from the people of another planet? What was their object? What had they to gain? ... Perhaps we were safe after all." The answer that destroyed all hope came to them borne in upon a wall of water that swept the British coast.

The telescopes of the world were centered now on just one object in the heavens. The bright evening star that adorned the western sky was the target for instruments great and small. It was past the half-moon phase now, and it became under magnification a gleaming crescent, a crescent that emitted from the dark sphere it embraced vivid flashes of light. Sykes' report had ample corroboration; the flash was seen by many, and it was repeated the next night and the next.

What was it? the waiting world asked. And the answer came not from the telescopes and their far-reaching gaze but from the waters of the Atlantic. In the full blaze of day came a meteor that swept to the earth in an arc of fire to outshine the sun. There must have been those who saw it strike—passengers and crews of passing ships—but its plunge into the depths of the Atlantic spelled death for each witness.

The earth trembled with the explosion that followed. A gas—some new compound that united with water to give volumes tremendous—that only could explain it. The ocean rose from its depths and flung wave after wave to race outward in circles of death.

Hundreds of feet in height at their source—this could only be estimated—they were devastating when they struck. The ocean raged over the frail bulwark of England in wave upon wave, and, retreating, the waters left smooth, shining rock where cities had been. The stone and steel of their buildings was scattered far over the desolate land or drawn in the suction of retreating waters to the sea.

Ireland, too, and France and Spain. Even the coast of America felt the shock of the explosion and was swept by tidal waves of huge proportions. But the coast of Britain took the blow at its worst.

The world was stunned and waiting—waiting!—when the next blow fell. The flashes were coming from Venus at regular intervals, just twenty hours and nineteen minutes apart. And with exactly the same time intervals the bolts arrived from space to lay waste the earth.

They struck where they would: the ocean again; the Sahara; in the mountains of China; the Pacific was thrown into fearful convulsions; the wheat fields of Canada trembled and vanished before a blast of flaming gas....

Twenty hours and nineteen minutes! Where it would strike, the next star-shell, no man might say; that it surely would come was a deadly and nerve-shattering certainty. The earth waited and prayed under actual bombardment.

Some super-gun, said science with conviction; a great bore in the planet itself, perhaps. But it was fixed, and the planet itself aimed with an accuracy that was deadly; aimed once as each revolution brought its gun on the target. Herein, said science, lay a basis for hope.

If, in that distant world, there was only one such bore, it must be altering its aim as the planet approached; the gun must cease to bear upon the earth. And the changing sweep of the missiles' flight confirmed their belief.

Each meteor-shell that came rushing into Earth's embrace burned brilliantly as it tore into the air. And each flaming arc was increasingly bent, until—twenty hours and nineteen minutes had passed—twenty minutes—thirty—another hour ... and the peoples of Earth dropped humbly to their knees in thankful prayer, or raised vengeful eyes and clenched fists toward the heavens while their quivering lips uttered blasphemous curses. The menace, for the time, had passed; the great gun of Venus no longer was aiming toward the earth.

"No more ships," was the belief; "not this time." And the world turned to an accounting of its losses, and to wonder—wonder—what the planet's return would bring. A year and one half was theirs; one year and a half in which to live in safety, in which to plan and build.

A column, double leaded, in the *London Times* voiced the feeling of the world. It was copied and broadcast everywhere.

"Another attack," it concluded, "is not a probability—it is a certainty. They are destroying us for some reason known only to themselves. Who can doubt that when the planet returns there will be a further bombardment; an invasion by armed forces in giant ships; bombs dropped from them miles high in the air. This is what we must look forward to—death and destruction dealt out by a force we are unable to meet.

"Our munitions factories may build larger guns, but can they reach the heights at which these monster ships of space will lie, with any faint probability of inflicting damage? It is doubtful.

"Our aircraft is less than useless; its very name condemns it as inept. Craft of the air!—and we have to war against space ships which can rise beyond the thin envelope of gas that encircles the earth.

"The world is doomed—utterly and finally doomed; it is the end of humankind; slavery to a conquering race at the very best, unless—

"Let us face the facts fairly. It is war—war to the death—between the inhabitants of this world and of that other. We are men. What they are God alone can say. But they are creatures of mind as are we; what they have done, we may do.

"There is our only hope. It is vain, perhaps—preposterous in its assumption—but our sole and only hope. We must meet the enemy and defeat him, and we must do it on his own ground. To destroy their fleet we must penetrate space; to silence their deadly bombardment we must go out into space as they have done, reach their distant world as they have reached ours, and conquer as we would have been conquered.

"It is a tenuous hope, but our only one. Let our men of mundane warfare do their best—it will be useless. But if there be one spark of God-given genius in the world that can point the way to victory, let those in authority turn no deaf ear.

"It is a battle now of minds, and the best minds will win. Humanity—all humankind—is facing the end. In less than one year and a half we must succeed—or perish. And unless we conquer finally and decisively, the story of man in the history of the universe will be a tale that is told, a record of life in a book that is ended—closed—and forgotten through all eternity."

CHAPTER VII

A breath of a lethal gas shot from the flying ship had made Captain Blake as helpless as if every muscle were frozen hard, and he had got it only lightly, mixed with the saving blast of oxygen. His heart had gone on, and his breathing, though it became shallow, did not cease; he was even able to turn his eyes. But to the men in the observatory room the gas from the weapons of the attacking force came as a devastating, choking cloud that struck them senseless as if with a blow. Lieutenant McGuire hardly heard the sound of his own pistol before unconsciousness took him.

It was death for the men who were left—for them the quick darkness never lifted—but for McGuire and his companion there was reprieve.

He was lying flat on a hard floor when remembrance crept slowly back to his benumbed brain. An odor, sickish-sweet, was in his nostrils; the breath of life was being forcibly pumped and withdrawn from laboring lungs; a mask was tight against his face. He struggled to throw it off, and someone bending over removed it.

Someone! His eyes stared wonderingly at the grotesque face like a lingering phantasm of fevered dreams. There were others, he saw, and they were working over a body not far away upon the floor. He recognized the figure of Professor Sykes. Short, stocky, his clothes disheveled—but Sykes, unmistakably, despite the mask upon his face.

He, too, revived as McGuire watched, and, like the flyer, he looked wonderingly about him at his strange companions. The eyes of the two met and held in wordless communication and astonishment.

The unreal creatures that hovered near withdrew to the far side of the room. The walls beyond them were of metal, white and gleaming; there were doorways. In another wall were portholes—round windows of thick glass that framed circles of absolute night. It was dark out beyond them with a blackness that was relieved only by sharp pin-points of brilliance—stars in a night sky such as McGuire had never seen.

Past and present alike were hazy to the flyer; the spark of life had been brought back to his body from a far distance; there was time needed to part the unreal from the real in these new and strange surroundings.

There were doorways in the ceiling, and others in the floor near where he lay; ladders fastened to the wall gave access to these doors. A grotesque figure appeared above the floor and, after a curious glance at the two men, scrambled into the room and vanished through the opening in the ceiling. It was some time before the significance of this was plain to the wondering man—before he reasoned that he was in the enemy ship, aimed outward from the earth, and the pull of gravitation and the greater force of the vessel's constant acceleration held its occupants to the rear walls of each room. That lanky figure had been making its way forward toward the bow of the ship. McGuire's mind was clearing; he turned his attention now to the curious, waiting creatures, his captors.

There were five of them standing in the room, five shapes like men, yet curiously, strangely, different. They were tall of stature, narrow across the shoulders, muscular in a lean, attenuated fashion. But their faces! McGuire found his eyes returning in horrified fascination to each hideous, inhuman countenance.

A colorless color, like the dead gray of ashes; a skin like that of an African savage from which all but the last vestige of color had been drained. It was transparent, parchment-like, and even in the light of the room that glowed from some hidden source, he could see the throbbing lines of blood-vessels that showed livid through the translucent skin. And he remembered, now, the fingers, half-seen in his moments of awakening—they were like clinging tendrils, colorless, too, in that ashy gray, and showed the network of veins as if each hand had been flayed alive.

The observer found himself analyzing, comparing, trying to find some earthly analogy for these unearthly creatures. Why did he think of potatoes sprouting in a cellar? What possible connection had these half-human things with that boyhood recollection? And he had seen some laboratory experiments with plants and animals that had been cut off from the sunlight—and now the connection was clear; he knew what this idea was that was trying to form.

These were creatures of the dark. These bleached, drained faces showed skin that had never known the actinic rays of the sun; their whole framework proclaimed the process that had been going on through countless generations. Here was a race that had lived, if not in absolute darkness, then in some place where sunlight never shone—a place of half-light—or of clouds.

"Clouds!" The exclamation was startled from him. And: "Clouds!" he repeated meditatively; he was seeing again a cloud-wrapped world in the eye-piece of a big refracting telescope. "Blanketed in clouds," Professor Sykes had said. The scientist himself was speaking to him now in bewildered tones.

"Clouds?" he inquired. "That's a strange remark to make. Where are we, Lieutenant McGuire? I remember nothing after you fired. Are we flying—in the clouds?"

"A long, long way beyond them, is my guess," said McGuire grimly. It was staggering what all this might mean; there was time needed for fuller comprehension. But the lean bronzed face of the flyer flushed with animation, and in spite of the terrors that must surely lie ahead he felt strangely elated at the actuality of an incredible adventure.

Slowly he got to his feet to find that his muscles still were reluctant to respond to orders; he helped the professor to arise. And from the group that drew back further into the far end of the room came a subdued and rasping tumult of discordant sound.

One, seemingly in charge, held a weapon in his hand, a slender tube no thicker than a common wire; and ending in a cylinder within the creature's hand. He pointed it in threatening fashion while his voice rose in a shrill call. McGuire and Professor Sykes stood quiet and waited for what the next moment might have in store, but McGuire waved the weapon aside in a gesture that none could fail to read.

"Steady," he told his companion. "We're in a ticklish position. Do nothing to alarm them."

From up above them came an answering shrill note. Another of the beings was descending into the room.

"Ah!" said Lieutenant McGuire softly, "the big boss, himself. Now let's see what will happen."

If there had seemed something of timidity in the repulsive faces of the waiting creatures, this newcomer was of a different type. He opened flabby thin lips to give one sharp note of command. It was as sibilant as the hissing of a snake. The man with the weapon returned it to a holder at his side; the whole group cringed before the power and authority of the new arrival.

The men that they had seen thus far were all garbed alike; a loose-fitting garment of one piece that was ludicrously like the play rompers that children might wear. These were dull red in color, the red of drying blood, made of strong woven cloth. But this other was uniformed differently.

McGuire noted the fineness of the silky robe. Like the others this was made of one piece, loosely fitting, but its bright vivid scarlet made the first seem drab and dull. A belt of metal about his waist shone like gold and matched the emblem of precious metal in the turban on his head.

All this the eyes of the flyer took in at a glance; his attention was only momentarily diverted from the ashen face with eyes narrow and slitted, that stared with the cold hatred of a cat into those of the men.

He made a sound with a whistling breath. It seemed to be a question directed to them, but the import of it was lost.

"An exceedingly queer lot," Professor Sykes observed. "And this chap seems distinctly hostile."

"He's no friend of mine," said McGuire as the thin, pendulous lips repeated their whistling interrogation.

"I can't place them," mused the scientist. "Those facial characteristics.... But they must be of some nationality, speak some tongue."

He addressed himself to the figure with the immobile, horrid face.

"We do not understand you," he said with an ingratiating smile. "*Comprenez vous Francaise?... Non?*"... German, perhaps, or Spanish?... "*Sprecken sie Deutsche? Usted habla Española?...*"

He followed with a fusillade of questions in strange and varying tongues. "I've even tried him with Chinese," he protested in bewilderment and stared amazed at his companion's laughter.

There had to be a reaction from the strain of the past hours, and Lieutenant McGuire found the serious questioning in polyglot tongues and the unchanging feline stare of that hideous face too much for his mental restraint. He held his sides, while he shook and roared with laughter beyond control, and the figure before him glared with evident disapproval of his mirth.

There was a hissing order, and two figures from the corner sprang forward to seize the flyer with long clinging fingers. Their strength he had overestimated, for a violent throw of his body twisted him free, and his outstretched hands sent the two sprawling across the room. Their leader took one quick step forward, then paused as if hesitating to meet this young adversary.

"Do go easy," Professor Sykes was imploring. "We do not know where we are nor who they are, but we must do nothing to antagonize them."

McGuire had reacted from his hilarious seizure with an emotional swing to the opposite extreme. "I'll break their damn necks," he growled, "if they get rough with me." And his narrow eyes exchanged glare for glare with those in the face like blood and ashes before him.

The cold cat eyes held steadily upon him while the scarlet figure retreated. A louder call, shrill and vibrant, came from the thin lips, and a swarm of bodies in dull red were scrambling into the room to mass about their scarlet leader. Above and behind them the face under its brilliant turban and golden clasp was glaring in triumph.

The tall figures crouched, grotesque and awkward; their long arms and hands with grasping, tendril-like fingers were ready. McGuire waited for the sharp hissing order that would throw these things upon him, and he met the attack when it came with his own shoulders dropped to the fighter's pose, head drawn in close and both fists swinging free.

There were lean fingers clutching at his throat, a press of blood-red bodies thick about him, and a clustering of faces where color blotched and flowed.

The thud of fists in blows that started from the floor was new to these lean creatures that clawed and clung like cats. But they trampled on those who went down before the flyer's blows and stood upon them to spring at his head; they crowded in in overwhelming numbers while their red hands tore and twined about his face.

It was no place now for long swings; McGuire twisted his body and threw his weight into quick short jabs at the faces before him. He was clear for an instant and swung his heavy boot at something that clung to one leg; then met with a rain of hooks and short punches the faces that closed in again. He saw in that instant a wild whirl of bodies where the stocky figure of Professor Sykes was smothered beneath his taller antagonists. But the professor, if he was forgetting the science of the laboratory, was remembering that of the squared circle—and the battle was not entirely one sided.

McGuire was free; the blood was trickling down his face from innumerable cuts where sharp-nailed fingers had sunk deep. He wiped the red stream from his eyes and threw himself at the weaving mass of bodies that eddied about Sykes in frantic struggle across the room.

The face of the professor showed clear for a moment. Like McGuire he was bleeding, and his breath came in short explosive gasps, but he was holding his own! The eyes of McGuire glimpsed a wildly gesticulating, shouting figure in the rear. The face, contorted with rage, was almost the color of the brilliant scarlet that the creature wore. The blood-stained man in khaki left his companion to fight his own battle, and plunged headlong at a leaping cluster of dull red, smashed through with a frenzied attack of straight rights and lefts, and freed himself to make one final leap at the leader of this unholy pack.

He was fighting in blind desperation now; the two were out-numbered by the writhing, lean-bodied creatures, and this thing that showed in blurred crimson before him was the directing power of them all. The figure symbolized and personified to the raging man all the repulsive ugliness of the leaping horde. The face came clear before him through the mist of blood, and he put the last ounce of his remaining strength and every pound of weight behind a straight, clean drive with his right fist.

His last conscious impression was of a red, clawing hand that was closed around the thick butt of a tube of steel ... then down, and still down, he plunged into a bottomless pit of whirling, red flashes and choking fumes....

There were memories that were to occur to Lieutenant McGuire afterward—visions, dim and hazy and blurred, of half-waking moments when strange creatures forced food and water into his mouth, then held a mask upon his face while he resisted weakly the breathing of sweet, sickly fumes that sent him back to unconsciousness.

There were many such times; some when he came sufficiently awake to know that Sykes was lying near him, receiving similar care. Their lives were being preserved: How, or why, or what life might hold in store he neither knew nor cared; the mask and the deep-drawn fumes brought stupor and numbness to his brain.

A window was in the floor beside him when he awoke—a circular window of thick glass or quartz. But no longer did it frame a picture of a sky in velvet blackness; no unwinking pin-points of distant stars pricked keenly through the night; but, clear and dazzling, came a blessed radiance that could mean only sunshine. A glowing light that was dazzling to his sleep-filled eyes, it streamed in golden—beautiful—to light the unfamiliar room and show motionless upon the floor the figure of Professor Sykes. His torn clothing had been neatly arranged, and his face showed livid lines of healing cuts and bruises.

McGuire tried gingerly to move his arms and legs; they were still functioning though stiff and weak from disuse. He raised himself slowly and stood swaying on his feet, then made his uncertain way to his companion and shook him weakly by the shoulder.

Professor Sykes breathed deeply and raised leaden lids from tired eyes to stare uncomprehendingly at McGuire. Soon his dark pupils ceased to dilate, and he, too, could see their prison and the light of day.

"Sunlight!" he said in a thin voice, and he seemed to know now that they were in the air; "I wonder—I wonder—if we shall land—what country? ... Some wilderness and a strange race—a strange, strange race!"

He was muttering half to himself; the mystery of these people whom he could not identify was still troubling him.

McGuire helped the other man to his feet, and they clung to each to the other for support as they crossed to kneel beside the floor-window and learn finally where their captors meant to take them.

A wilderness, indeed, the sight that met their eyes, but a wilderness of clouds—no unfamiliar sight to Lieutenant McGuire of the United States Army air service. But to settle softly into them instead of driving through with glistening wings—this was new and vastly different from anything he had known.

Sounds came to them in the silence, penetrating faintly through thick walls—the same familiar wailing call that trembled and quavered and seemed to the listening men to be guiding them down through the mist.

Gone was the sunlight, and the clouds beyond the deep-set window were gloriously ablaze with a brilliance softly diffused. The cloud bank was deep, and they felt the craft under them sink slowly, steadily into the misty embrace. It thinned below them to drifting vapor, and the first hazy shadows of the ground showed through from far beneath. Their altitude, the flyer knew, was still many thousands of feet.

"Water," said McGuire, as his trained eyes made plain to him what was still indistinct to the scientist. "An ocean—and a shore-line—" More clouds obscured the view; they parted suddenly to show a portion only of a clear-cut map.

It stretched beyond the confines of their window, that unfamiliar line of wave-marked shore; the water was like frozen gold, wrinkled in countless tiny corrugations and reflecting the bright glow from above. But the land,—that drew their eyes!

Were those cities, those shadow-splashed areas of gray and rose?... The last veiling clouds dissolved, and the whole circle was plain to their view.

The men leaned forward, breathless, intent, till the scientist, Sykes—the man whose eyes had seen and whose brain recorded a dim shape in the lens of a great telescope—Sykes drew back with a quivering, incredulous breath. For below them, so plain, so unmistakable, there lay an island, large even from this height, and it formed on this round map a sharp angle like a great letter "L."

"We shall know that if we ever see it again," Professor Sykes had remarked in the quiet and security of that domed building surmounting the heights of Mount Lawson. But he said nothing now, as he stared at his companion with eyes that implored McGuire to arouse him from this sleep, this dream that could never be real. But McGuire, lieutenant one-time in the forces of the U. S. A., had seen it too, and he stared back with a look that gave dreadful confirmation.

The observatory—Mount Lawson—the earth!—those were the things unreal and far away. And here before them, in brain-stunning actuality, were the markings unmistakable—the markings of Venus. And they were landing, these two, in the company of creatures wild and strange as the planet—on Venus itself!

(To be continued.)

IN THE NEXT ISSUE

THE APE-MEN OF XLOTLI

A Thrilling Novelette of the Nether World

By David R. Sparks

GRAY DENIM

A Story of the Future

By Harl Vincent

SLAVES OF THE DUST

An Amazing Story of Bio-Chemical Achievement and Revenge

By Sophie Wenzel Ellis

THE PIRATE PLANET

Part Two of the Breath-Taking Current Novel

By Charles W. Diffin

—And Others!

"The connection is made," murmured Von Stein.

THE DESTROYER

By William Merriam Rouse

The pencil in the hand of Allen Parker refused to obey his will. A strange unseen force pushed his will aside and took possession of the pencil point so that what he drew was not his own. It was the same when he turned from drawing board to typewriter. The sentences were not of his framing; the ideas were utterly foreign to him. This was the first hint he received of the fate that was drawing in like night upon him and his beautiful wife.

> Slowly, insidiously, there stole over Allen Parker something uncanny. He could no longer control his hands—even his brain!

Parker, a young writer of growing reputation who illustrated his own work, was making a series of pencil sketches for a romance partly finished. The story was as joyous and elusive as sunlight, and until to-day his sketches had held the same quality. Now he could not tap the reservoir from which he had taken the wind-blown hair and smiling eyes of Madelon, his heroine.

When he drew or wrote he seemed to be submerged in the dark waters of a measureless evil pit. The face that mocked him from the paper was stamped with a world-old knowledge of forbidden things.

Parker dropped his pencil and leaned back, tortured. He and his wife, Betty, had taken this house in Pine Hills, a small and extremely quiet suburban village, solely for the purpose of concentration on the book which was to be the most important work he had done. He went to the door of the room that he used for a studio and called:

"Betty! Can you come here a moment, please?"

There was a patter of running feet on the stairs and then a girl of twenty, or thereabout, came into the room. Any man would have said she was a blessing. Her hair "was yellow like ripe corn," and her vivid blue eyes held depth and character and charm.

"Look!" exclaimed Parker. "What do you think of this stuff?"

For a moment there was silence. Then Allen Parker saw something he had never before seen in his wife's face for him or his work—a look of complete disgust.

"I wouldn't have believed you capable of doing anything so ... so horrid!" she said coldly. "How could you?"

"I don't know!" His arms, which had been ready to take her to him for comfort, dropped. "The work has been ... difficult, lately. As though something were pulling at my mind. But not like this! It isn't *me*!"

"It must be you, since it came out of you!" She turned away and moved restlessly to one of the windows.

"Through me!" muttered Parker. "Ideas *come*!"

"You'll have to do something!"

"But what? I don't know what to do!"

"Why not go to see that new doctor?" asked Betty, over her shoulder. "Dr. Friedrich von Stein?"

"Von Stein?" repeated Parker, vaguely. "Don't know him. Anyhow, I don't need a doctor. What in the world made you think of that?"

"Nothing, except that I can see his house from here. He's taken what they call 'the old Reynolds place.' You know—opposite the church. We looked at it and thought it was too large for us. He's made a lot of alterations."

"Oh, yes!" Parker had placed the newcomer, more recent than himself. "I had an idea that he was a doctor of philosophy, not medicine."

"He has half a dozen degrees, they say. Certainly he's a stunning looking man. I saw him on the street."

"Maybe he doesn't practice." The artist was gazing, baffled and sick at heart, upon what he had wrought. "And what could he do, unless it's my liver?"

"He might be a psycho-analyst, or something like that," she replied, slowly.

"But why the wild interest in this particular doctor?" Parker roused himself and looked at her. He felt irritable, and was ashamed of it.

"Only for your work," said Betty. A faint pink touched her cheeks.

Allen Parker had a sudden feeling of certainty that his wife was lying to him. To one who knew the Parkers it would have been equally impossible to think of Betty as lying, or of her husband as believing such a thing. Parker was outraged by his own suspicion. He sprang up and began to pace the floor.

"All right, then!" he exploded. "My work is going to the dogs! Why, there's an appointment with Cartwright to-morrow to show him these sketches, and the last few chapters I've done! We'll go now! If this man can't do anything for me I'll try somebody else!"

In ten minutes they were walking up the quiet street toward the present home of Dr. Friedrich von Stein. Despite his self-absorption Parker could not help noticing that his wife had never looked more attractive than she did at this moment. Her color had deepened, little wisps of hair curled against her cheeks, and there was a sparkle in her eyes which he knew came only on very particular occasions.

Even from the outside it was apparent that many strange things had been done to the staid and dignified house of Reynolds. A mass of aerials hung above the roof. Some new windows had been cut at the second floor and filled with glass of a peculiar reddish-purple tinge. A residence had been turned into a laboratory, in sharp contrast to the charming houses up and down the street and the church of gray stone that stood opposite.

Beside the door, at the main entrance, a modest plate bore the legend: "Dr. Friedrich von Stein." Parker pressed the bell. Then he squared his broad shoulders and waited: a very miserable, very likeable young man, with a finely shaped head and a good set of muscles under his well cut clothes. He had brought his sketches, but he was uncomfortable with the portfolio under his arm. It seemed to contaminate him.

The door opened to reveal a blocky figure of a man in a workman's blouse and overalls. The fellow was pale of eye, towheaded; he appeared to be good natured but of little intelligence. The only remarkable thing about him was a livid welt that ran across one cheek, from nose to ear. Beside him a glossy-coated dachshund wagged furiously, after having barked once as a matter of duty.

"May we see Dr. von Stein?" asked Parker. "If he is in?"

"I will ask the Herr Doktor if he iss in," replied the man, stiffly.

"*Dummkopf!*" roared a voice from inside the house. An instant later man and dog shrank back along the hall and there appeared in their place one of the most striking personalities Allen Parker had ever seen.

Dr. Friedrich von Stein was inches more than six feet tall and he stood perfectly erect, with the unmistakable carriage of a well drilled soldier. He was big boned, but lean, and every movement was made with military precision. More than any other feature his eyes impressed Parker: they were steady, penetrating, and absolutely black. But for a thread of gray here and there his well-kept beard and hair were black. He might have been any age from forty to sixty, so deceptive was his appearance.

"Come in, if you please," he said, before Parker could speak. Von Stein's voice was rich and deep, but with a metallic quality which somehow corresponded with his mechanical smile. Except for the guttural r's there was hardly a hint of the foreigner in his speech. "It is Mr. and Mrs. Parker, I believe? I am Dr. von Stein."

He stood aside for them to pass into the hallway, and while they murmured their thanks he shot a volley of German at the man, whom he called Heinrich. The frightened servant vanished; and the Parkers were taken into a living room furnished carelessly, but in good enough taste. Betty took her place on a couch, to which the doctor led her with a bow. Parker sank into an overstuffed chair not far from a window.

"I learned your names because of the beauty of madame," said Von Stein, as he stood looming above the mantel. Again he bowed. "One could not see her without wishing to know how such a charming woman was called. You are my neighbors from down the street, I believe."

"Yes," replied Allen. He wanted to be agreeable, but found it difficult. "And I think Mrs. Parker has developed a great admiration for you. She persuaded me to come here to-day. Are you, by chance, a psycho-analyst? I don't even know that you are a doctor of medicine, but—"

"I know a very great deal about the human mind," interrupted Dr. von Stein calmly. "I know a great deal about many things. I am not going to practice medicine here in Pine Hills because I have research work to do, but I will help you if I can. What is your trouble?"

The question brought back to Parker the mood of half an hour ago. Almost savagely he snapped the portfolio open and spread out a few of his recent drawings, with some of the earlier ones for comparison.

"Look!" he cried. "These vicious things are what I am doing now! I can't help myself! The pencil does not obey me! Apparently I have no emotional control. It's as though my normal ideas were shouldered aside, like people in a crowd. And my writing to-day was as bad as these illustrations. I'm doing a book. Consider these things carefully, Doctor. They are not obscene, except by inference. They can't be censored. The book would go through the mails. Yet they are deadly! Look at my heroine in these two pictures. In one she is like—like violets! In the other she looks capable of any crime! What is she? A vampire, if there is such a thing? A witch? I can almost believe in demonology since I made these last drawings!"

Parker, in spite of his excitement, tried to read the face of Dr. Friedrich von Stein. He found nothing but the automatic smile upon that mask. Yet it seemed to the artist that this time there was a hint of real pleasure in the curve of the lips. Was it possible that anyone could like those drawings? Parker began to think that he was going insane.

"This is most unfortunate for you," rumbled the doctor. "I understand. But I trust that the condition can be remedied, if it persists. You, Mr. Parker, and you, Madame, do you understand something of physics, of psychology, of metaphysics?"

"I fear that I'm rather ignorant," answered Betty. "Certainly I am in comparison with a man of your attainments."

Dr. von Stein bowed. He turned his black eyes upon Parker.

"And you, sir? I must adjust my explanation to—what shall I say? To your knowledge of the higher reaches of scientific thought?"

"Why, I majored in philosophy in college," said Parker, hesitatingly. "But that's quite a time ago, Herr Doktor. Of course I've tried to keep up with the conclusions of science. But a writer or a painter doesn't have any too much opportunity. He has his own problems to concern him."

"Yes, indeed!" Dr. von Stein was thoughtful. "So, and especially for the benefit of madame, I shall speak in terms of the concrete."

"Please consider me stupid!" begged Betty. "But I want to understand!"

"Certainly, except that you are not stupid, Madame. I will proceed. Both of you, I assume, know something of the radio? Very good! You know that an etheric wave transmits the message, and that it is received and amplified so that it is within the range of the human ear. These waves were there when paleolithic man hunted his meat with a stone-tipped club. To use them it was necessary to invent the microphone, and a receiving instrument.

"What I have said you already know. But here is what may startle you. Human thought is an etheric wave of the same essential nature as the radio wave. They are both electrical currents external to man. Thoughts sweep across the human mind as sound currents sweep across the aerials of a radio—"

"I told you!" Allen Parker turned a triumphant face to his wife. "Pardon me, Herr Doktor! I have tried to convince Mrs. Parker that my idea came from outside!"

“Exactly!" Dr. von Stein took no offense. "And a difference between the mind and the radio set is that with the radio you tune in upon whatever you choose, and when you choose. The mind is not under such control, although it should be. It receives that to which it happens to be open. Or that thought which has been intensified and strengthened by having been received and entertained by other minds. In India they say: 'Five thousand died of the plague and fifty thousand died of fear.' Do you both follow me?"

It was unnecessary to ask. Betty sat on the edge of the couch, intent upon every word. Parker, although more restrained, was equally interested. Moreover he was delighted to have what he had felt instinctively confirmed, in a way, by a man of science.

"Herbert Spencer said," continued the doctor, "that no thought, no feeling, is ever manifested save as the result of a physical force. This principle will before long be a scientific commonplace. And Huxley predicted that we would arrive at a mechanical equivalent of consciousness. But I will not attempt to bolster my position with authorities. I know, and I can prove what I know.

"You, Mr. Parker, have been receiving some particularly annoying thoughts which have been intensified, it may be, by others, or another. Human will power can alter the rate of vibration of the line of force, or etheric wave. So-called good thoughts have a high rate of vibration, and those which are called bad ordinarily have a low rate. Have you, perhaps, an enemy?"

"Not that I know of," replied Parker, in a low voice.

"Then it would follow that this is accidental."

“Good heavens! Do you mean to say that someone could do this to me maliciously?"

"So far my experiments leave something to be desired," said Dr. von Stein, without answering directly. "No doubt you are peculiarly susceptible to thoughts which bear in any way on your work."

"But isn't there any help for it?" asked Betty. She was regarding her husband with the eyes of a stranger.

"I believe I can do something for Mr. Parker."

There was a knock at the door. The doctor boomed an order to come in. Heinrich, with the dachshund at his heels, entered bearing a tray with a bottle of wine and some slices of heavy fruit cake. He drew out a table and placed the tray.

"Do not bring that dog in when I have guests," said Von Stein. He spoke with a gleam of white teeth. "You know what will happen, Heinrich?"

"*Ja*, Herr Doktor! I take Hans oudt!" The man was terrified. He gathered the dog into his arms and fairly fled from the room. Dr. von Stein turned with a smile.

"I have to discipline him," he explained. "He's a stupid fellow, but faithful. I can't have ordinary servants about. There are scientific men who would be willing to bribe them for a look at my laboratory."

"I did not know such things were done among scholars," said Betty, slowly.

"What I have accomplished means power, Madame!" exclaimed the doctor. "There are jackals in every walk of life. If an unscrupulous man of science got into my laboratory, a physicist for instance, he might ... find out things!"

Dr. von Stein turned to his duties as host. He filled their glasses, and watched with satisfaction Betty's obvious enjoyment of the cake. A box of mellow Havanas appeared from a cabinet: imported cigarettes from a smoking stand. But Parker, in spite of a liking for good wine and tobacco, was far too much concerned about his work to forget the errand that had brought him there.

"So you think," he said, when there was opportunity, "that you can help me, Dr. von Stein?"

"I can," replied von Stein, firmly; "but before attempting anything I'd like to wait a day or two. The attacking thoughts may become less violent, or your resistance greater, in either of which cases the condition will fade out. You will either get better or much worse. If you are worse come to see me again, and I promise you that I will do something!"

"I'll come, and thank you!" Parker felt better, and more cheerful than he had since the beginning of the disturbance. "Few things could make me suffer so much as trouble with my work."

"That is what I thought," agreed Dr. von Stein.

Betty rose. Her husband caught the look in her eyes as they met the bright, black gaze of Dr. von Stein, and he went cold. That look had always been for him alone. Her feet seemed to linger on the way to the door.

"He's wonderful!" she breathed, as they started down the uneventful street. "Scientific things never interested me before. But he makes them vital, living!"

"And yet," said Parker, thoughtfully, "there's something uncanny about that man!"

"Nonsense!" exclaimed Betty. "It's because he's a genius! Don't be small, Allen!"

Parker gasped, and remained silent. He could not remember that his wife had ever spoken to him in quite that way. They finished the little journey home without speaking again and Parker went directly to studio. He sat down, with drooping shoulders, and considered the mess he had made of his book. Well, there was nothing to do but see Cartwright to-morrow and face the music!

Dinner that night was a mournful affair. The soft footsteps of the servant going in and out of the dining room, the ticking of the clock, were almost the only sounds. Betty was deep in her own thoughts; Parker was too miserable to talk. He went to bed early and lay staring into the darkness for what seemed like an eternity of slow moving hours.

The tall, deep voiced clock in the hall downstairs had just struck one when suddenly Parker's room was flooded with light. He sat up, blinking, and saw Betty standing near his bed. Her fingers twisted against each other; her face was drawn and white.

"Allen!" she whispered. "I'm afraid!"

Instantly he was on his feet; his arms went around her and the yellow head dropped wearily against his shoulder.

"Afraid of what?" he cried. "What is it, sweetheart?"

"I don't know!" All at once her body stiffened and she pulled away from him. Then she laughed—"What nonsense! I must have been having a bad dream ... it's nothing. Sorry I bothered you, Allen!"

She was gone before his could stop her. Bewildered, he did not know whether to follow. Better not, he thought. She would sleep now, and perhaps he would. But he was worried. Betty was becoming less and less like herself.

At last Parker did sleep, to awake shortly after daylight. He got a hasty breakfast and took an early train to New York. When John Cartwright, a shrewd and kindly man well advanced in years, arrived at his office Allen Parker was right there waiting for him.

Cartwright had shown a real affection for the younger man, a paternal interest. He beamed, as usual, until he sat down with the new drawings. Slowly the smile faded from his face. He went over them twice, three times, and then he looked up.

"My boy," he said, "did you do these?"

"Yes."

"Do you know that you are turning a delicate and beautiful romance into a lascivious libel on the human race?"

"It is being done," replied Parker, in a low voice. "And I—I can't help myself!"

"What do you mean by that?"

"I mean that when I start to draw Madelon my hand produces that woman of Babylon! The writing is just as bad. It's full of sneering hints, double meanings ... I shall destroy the stuff. I've been to see a psycho-analyst."

"Ah!" thoughtfully. "Perhaps you're tired, Allen. Why not take Betty for a sea trip? There'll still be time for fall publication."

"I'm going to try everything possible. I'd rather be dead than do work like this!"

When Parker left his friend he was somewhat encouraged. After the first shock Cartwright had been inclined to make light of the difficulty, and by the time Allen Parker reached Pine Hills his stride had the usual swing and snap.

He ran up the steps of his house and burst into the living room with a smile. Betty was sitting by one of the windows, her hands lying relaxed in her lap. She turned a somber face toward her husband, and spoke before he had time to say a word of greeting.

"You knew that Cordelia Lyman died a short time ago, didn't you?"

"What's that?" exclaimed Parker, bewildered. "Lyman? Oh, the old lady down the street who left her money to found a home for aged spinsters? What about it?"

"But she didn't leave her money to found a home for aged spinsters, Allen. She had said she was going to, and everybody thought so. Her will was admitted to probate, or whatever they call it, yesterday. She left half a million, all she had, to Dr. Friedrich von Stein, to be used as he thinks best for the advancement of science!"

"Good heavens!" Parker stared. "Why, I didn't know she knew him. He'd only been here a week or so when she died."

"There isn't a flaw in the will, they say. You can imagine that Pine Hills is talking!"

"Well," said Parker philosophically, "he's lucky. I hope he does something with it."

"He will," replied Betty, with conviction. "He'll do a great many things!"

Parker told her of his interview with Cartwright, but she seemed little interested. He did not try to work that day but, after he had put the offending drawings and manuscript out of sight, he wandered, read, smoked, and in the evening persuaded Betty to take a moonlight walk with him.

They passed the house of Dr. von Stein, from which came a faint humming that sounded like a dynamo. Across the street the church was alight for some service. Triumphant music drifted to them. The moon hung above the spire, with its cross outlined darkly against the brilliant sky. The windows were great jewels. Betty drew a deep breath.

"Sometimes, Allen," she said, "I feel like praying!"

"You *are* a beautiful prayer," whispered Parker.

She walked close to him, holding his arm, and repeated softly:

"Are not two prayers a perfect strength?And shall I feel afraid?"

But that was the end of that mood. By the time they arrived home Betty was again the strange, aloof, cold, slightly hard woman of the past few days. Again depression settled upon Allen Parker.

The next morning he breakfasted alone and went directly to the studio, without seeing Betty. Sun streamed into the room; the pencil moved swiftly. For a brief time Parker thought that he was himself again, as Madelon grew upon the block of paper. But the end was terrible. The last few strokes made her grotesque. This time the woman he had drawn was not merely evil; she was a mocking parody of his heroine. He threw drawing and pencil across the room.

But no real artist can be discouraged short of death. He went to work again and labored until luncheon time. The results were no better, although they varied. Now it seemed that some malevolent power was playing with him, torturing him to the accompaniment of devilish laughter. He was haggard and actually stooped of body when he bathed his face and went down to the dining room. From across the table Betty regarded him curiously.

"Fleming Proctor shot himself last night," she announced, calmly. "This morning they found him dead in his office."

"Proctor? You don't mean the president of the Pine Hills National Bank?"

"Yes." The expression of Betty's face did not change. "There was a note saying that he was sorry. It seems he'd made a large loan without security to an unknown person, and the bank examiner was coming to-day. Proctor said he couldn't help what he did. The note was confused as though he were trying to tell something and couldn't. They think his mind must have given way, particularly as they can't trace the loan, although the money is undoubtedly gone."

"That kind of thing doesn't happen!" Parker was stunned. He had known Fleming Proctor, and liked him. They met often at the country club. "Proctor was honest, and a fine business man!"

"It did happen, Allen!"

"I'd like to know more about it. That would have been a case for Dr. von Stein to take in hand."

"Perhaps," said Betty, in a voice like ice. "But I'm more interested in finding out how soon you are going to return to normal. Frankly, I'm beginning to get bored."

Without a word Parker rose and left the room. Never before had his wife hurt him like this. Doubly sensitive just now, he was suffering alone in the studio when the telephone rang.

"Dr. von Stein speaking. Are you better, Mr. Parker?"

"Worse! Much worse!"

"Then come to my house this evening at nine. May I expect you? And alone?"

"Yes." There was much Parker wanted to say, but he choked the words back. "I'll be there, and alone."

"I shall be ready for you. Good-by."

Allen Parker hung up the receiver. He did not leave the studio again until evening.

As Parker approached the house of Dr. Friedrich von Stein he saw that the church was lighted as it had been the night before. In a clear sky the moon rode above the spire. He paused to let his glance sweep up along the beautiful line that ran from earth to the slender cross. That was how he felt. He wanted to rise, as that line rose, from cumbering earth to clarity and beauty.

He mounted the steps and rang. Dr. von Stein met him, with eyes and teeth agleam in the hall light. Wearily Parker stepped inside. His mood of the moment before was fading.

"Go upstairs to my laboratory, if you please," said the doctor. "It is best that I see you there, for it may be that you will need treatment."

"I need something," replied Parker as he went up a long flight of stairs. "I'm in a bad way."

Without answer von Stein led him down a short corridor and held open a door. Allen Parker stepped into a room that bewildered him with its strange contrasts.

At a glance he saw that nearly the whole upper floor of the building had been converted into one gigantic room. Near a big stone fireplace, where burning driftwood sent up its many tinted flames, Heinrich stood rigidly at attention. Hans, the dachshund, crouched at his feet. When the dog started to meet Parker a guttural command stopped him.

Here there were bearskins on the floor, huge stuffed chairs, footrests, little tables, humidors, pipe racks, all that one could desire for comfort. Two German duelling swords were crossed above the mantel.

But beyond this corner everything was different. Parker saw the massed windows of reddish-purple glass; he saw apparatus for which he had no name, as well as some of the ordinary paraphernalia of the chemical laboratory. There was wiring everywhere, and a multitude of lighting fixtures. Utilitarian tables, desks and chairs were placed about with mathematical precision. There were plates and strips of metal set into the glass smooth flooring, which was broken by depressions and elevations of unusual form.

The most striking thing in the room was a huge copper bowl that hung inverted from the ceiling. In it, and extending down below the rim, was what seemed to be a thick and stationary mist. It looked as though the bowl had been filled with a silver gray mist and then turned bottom side up. But the cloud did not fall or float away.

"I can think and speak best from my desk," Von Stein was saying. "Please sit down facing me in the chair which Heinrich will place for you. Then we will talk."

Heinrich rolled one of the overstuffed chairs noiselessly to a position about six feet from the desk. Parker noticed a long metal strip in the floor between him and the doctor.

Just then Hans wriggled forward and the artist scratched his ears, to be rewarded by a grateful tongue. Again a command from Heinrich brought the dog to heel, but the voice was not so gruff this time. Together they returned to the fireplace.

Von Stein let his hands rest upon the desk top—a surface covered with levers, electric switches, push buttons, and contrivances the nature of which Parker could not guess. The doctor leaned forward. He threw over a switch. The lights in the room became less bright. He pressed a button. The Danse Macabre of Saint-Saens floated weirdly upon the air, as though the music came from afar off.

"Is that part of the treatment?" asked Parker, with a faint smile. "It's not cheering, exactly."

"Merely an idiosyncrasy of mine," answered Von Stein, showing his teeth. "Before anything is done I must, in order to aid the receptivity of your mind, go a little further with the explanation of certain things which I mentioned the other day. I promise not to bore you. More than that, Mr. Parker, I promise that you will be more interested than you have ever been in anything!"

It seemed to Parker that there was something sinister in the manner and speech of Dr. von Stein. The Dance of Death! Did that music have a meaning? Impossible! It was only his own sick mind that was allowing such thoughts to come to him.

"Anything that will help," he murmured.

"You have noticed that copper bowl?" Von Stein did not wait for a reply. "The misty appearance inside and underneath it is given by thousands upon thousands of minute platinum wires. When it is in use a slight electrical current is passed through it, varying in power according to the rate of vibration needed. That instrument, my dear sir, is a transmitter of thought. I may call it the microphone of the mind. I can tune in on any mind in the world, by experimenting up and down the vibration range to determine the susceptibility of the particular person. The human mind does not need an amplifier, as the radio receiving set does. Rather, it acts as its own amplifier, once having received the thought. I invented one, however, to prove that it could be done. I equipped Heinrich with it and in half an hour by suggestion reduced him to his present state of docile stupidity. I have, Mr. Parker, the means of moving people to do my bidding!"

Von Stein stopped abruptly, as though for emphasis and to allow his astounding statements to take effect. Parker sat stunned, struggling to grasp all the implications of what he had just heard. Suddenly they became clear. He saw events in order, and in relation to each other.

"So that's how it was with Cordelia Lyman!" he cried hoarsely, leaning forward. "And it was you who had that money from Fleming Proctor!"

"You are not unintelligent," remarked Dr. von Stein. "Better that science should have the Lyman money than a few old women of no particular use. As for Proctor, he was a fool. I would have protected him."

"And my pictures ... my book...."

"I can cure you, Mr. Parker. *If I will!*"

"And anyone is at the mercy of this man!" groaned Parker.

"Not absolutely, I'm sorry to say," said the doctor. "The action of thought on the human consciousness is exactly like that of sound on the tuning fork. When the mind is tuned right, we'll say for illustration, the lower vibrations are not picked out of the ether. But as few minds are tuned right, and as all vary from time to time, I'm practically omnipotent."

"You have changed the nature of my wife!" Parker was getting hold of himself and he could speak with a degree of calmness. "That is a worse crime than the one you've committed against me directly!"

"Mr. Parker," said the doctor, impressively, "you are in a web. I am the spider. You are the fly. I don't particularly desire to hurt you, but I want your wife. This is the crux of the matter. She is the woman to share my triumphs. Already I have aroused her interest. Give her up and you will continue your work as before. Refuse, and you will lose her just as certainly as though you give her to me. For, my dear sir, you will be insane in less than a month from now. I promise you that!"

Allen Parker was not one to indulge in melodrama. For a long moment he sat looking into the black eyes of Von Stein. Then he spoke carefully.

"If my wife of her own will loved you, and wanted freedom, I'd let her go. But this is a kind of hypnosis. It's diabolical!"

"Who but the devil was the father of magic?" asked the doctor, cheerfully. "Hypnosis is unconsciously based on a scientific principle which I have mastered. Repeated advertising of a tooth brush or a box of crackers is mild mental suggestion—hypnosis, if you will. My dear fellow, be sensible!"

"Sophistry!" growled Parker.

Von Stein laughed. He moved a lever upon a dial and a sheet of blue flame quivered between them. With another movement of the lever it vanished.

"I could destroy you instantly," he said, "and completely, and no one could prove a crime! I shall not do it. I have no time to be bothered with investigations. Think of the fate I have promised you. Think, and you will give her up!"

"I shall not!" Parker wiped cold drops from his forehead. The doctor frowned thoughtfully.

"I'll intensify her desire to come here to-night," he said. "She herself will persuade you."

Parker set his fingers into the arms of his chair as Von Stein rose and walked to the copper bowl. He stood directly under it, and put on goggles with shields fitting close to his feet. At the pressure of his foot a tablelike affair rose from the floor in front of him. This, like the desk, was equipped with numerous dials, buttons and levers. Von Stein manipulated them. The great cap of copper descended until his head was enveloped by the mist of platinum wires. A faint humming grew in the room. A tiny bell tinkled.

"The connection is made," murmured Von Stein. He lifted a hand for silence: then his fingers leaped among the gadgets on the table. After that came a brief period, measured by seconds, of immobility. Then the table sank from view, the copper bowl lifted, and Dr. von Stein went back to his chair.

"She will be here shortly," he said. "If that does not change your mind...."

He shrugged. Parker knew what that shrug meant. He searched his mind for a plan and found none. Better die fighting than yield, or risk the vengeance of Friedrich von Stein. If he could get the doctor away from the desk where he controlled the blue-white flame there might be a chance to do something. Von Stein was by far the larger man, but Parker had been an athlete all his life. If....

"That mass of copper and platinum," he said, tentatively, "will make you master of the world!"

"My brain, my intelligence, has made me master of the world!" corrected Von Stein, proudly. He was touched in the right spot now. "You have not seen all!"

He sprang up and went to one of the tables. From his pocket he took a piece of paper and crumpled it into a ball while, with the other hand, he made some electrical connections to a plate of metal set into the surface of the table. Next he placed the wad of paper on the plate. Then, standing at arm's length from the apparatus, he pressed a button. Instantly the paper disappeared behind a screen of the colors of the spectrum, from red to violet. The banded colors were there for a minute fraction of a second. Then there was nothing where the paper had been on the plate. Von Stein smiled as he stepped away from the table.

"The electron is formed by the crossing of two lines of force," he said, "and the interaction of positive and negative polarity. The electron is a stress in the ether, nothing more, but it is the stuff of which all matter is made. Thought is vibration in one dimension; matter in two. You have just seen me untie the knot, dissociate the electrons, or what you will. In plain language I have caused matter to vanish utterly. That paper is not burned up. It no longer exists in any form. The earth upon which we stand, Parker, can be dissolved like mist before the sun!"

Appalled as he was at this man who boasted and made good his terrible boasts Allen Parker had not forgotten the purpose that was in him. Now was his chance, while Von Stein stood smiling triumphantly between table and desk.

Parker shot from his chair with the speed of utter desperation. He feinted, and drove a vicious uppercut to the jaw of Dr. Friedrich von Stein. The doctor reeled but he did not go down. His fists swung. Parker found him no boxer, and beat a tattoo upon his middle. Von Stein began to slump.

Then two thick muscled arms closed around the artist from behind and he was lifted clear of the floor. He kicked, and tried to turn, but it was useless. The doctor recovered himself. His eyes blazed fury.

"Put him in the chair, Heinrich!" he roared. "For this I will show you what I can do, Herr Parker!"

At that instant little Hans, who had been yelping on the edge of the battle, dashed in. He leaped for the throat of Von Stein. The doctor kicked him brutally.

The shriek of agony from Hans loosened the arms of Heinrich. Parker got his footing again. He saw the clumsy serving man spring forward and gather his dog up to his breast. Again Parker rushed for his enemy.

It was clear now that Von Stein was cut off from the controls he wanted, and without Heinrich he could not master Parker in a fight. For an instant he stood baffled. Then he retreated the length of the room, taking what blows he could not beat off. He staggered upon a plate of metal set into the floor, righted himself, and failed in an attempt to catch hold of Parker. Suddenly he bowed in the direction of the distant doorway.

Allen half turned. Betty was coming down the room, staring and breathless.

"*Leben sie wohl!*" cried Von Stein. "Farewell, Madame! I should like to take you with me!"

A great flash of the colors of the spectrum sent Parker reeling back. Dr. Friedrich von Stein had gone the way of the crumpled ball of paper.

There was a long moment of silence. Then Allen Parker found his wife in his arms, clinging to him.

"'Are not two prayers a perfect strength?'" she murmured, sobbing against his heart.

A HUNDRED MILES UNDERGROUND

Scientists bidding their families good-by in the morning to drop fifty or a hundred miles underground in high speed elevators, there to undertake researches not possible nearer to the earth's surface, may be realities of the next decade or two if some wealthy individual or institution accepts the recommendation of Dr. Harlow Shapley, distinguished astronomer of Harvard, in a talk recently before the American Geographical Society.

The earth's interior, Dr. Shapley said, is the "third dimension" of geography. Exploration of the planet's surface soon must cease from lack of places to explore. Even the upper air is coming to be reasonably well known scientifically, thanks to instruments sent up with balloons and to the radio and other investigators who have been uncovering secrets of upper-air electricity. But the interior of the earth is still one of the great mysteries. It is a paradox of astronomy that much more is known about the center of the sun or a star like Sirius than about the center of the earth.

Deep shafts of bore holes into the earth have been suggested often as sources of heat for human use. It is doubtful, however, whether such heat supplies could be obtained. For one thing, the supposed internal heat of the earth is still nothing but a guess. It may be that the relatively slight increases of heat found as one goes deeper in existing mines are due to radioactivity in the rocks instead of to outward seepage from the internal fires. Another difficulty about utilizing earth heat is that heat moves so slowly through substances like rock, as any housewife can prove by trying to fry an egg on a brick placed over a gas flame. As soon as the rock heat immediately at the bottom of a bore hole had been exhausted heat supply would stop until more could diffuse in from the sides.

Dr. Shapley's suggestion, in any event, is not to search for heat but for facts. Even in existing, relatively shallow mines, he believes, scientific laboratories at different depths under the surface might yield valuable data not now obtainable. Most scientific men will agree. Revolutionary as the idea may seem to those familiar only with the standardized laboratories of physics or chemistry, there are sound reasons why a half-dozen or so of the sciences should do precisely what Dr. Shapley suggests.

At least one underground laboratory has already been installed, for Prof. E. B. Babcock of the University of California has such a workroom in the Twin Peaks Tunnel, underneath the mountain that rises above the city of San Francisco. Natural radioactivity in the rocks thereabouts is greater than normal and Prof. Babcock finds that this apparently increases new species among fruit flies.

To dig out laboratory rooms a mile or so down in existing deep mines probably would cost far less than many enterprises already financed by philanthropists. Even to deepen these shafts for several miles would be much less difficult than most people imagine.

Increasing heat, if it is found that heat does increase, would not be difficult to overcome had the engineers sufficient money. Ventilation and transportation to and from the surface, while too costly for the business enterprise of winning metals from very deep mines, probably would present no serious difficulty were facts the chief object instead of profit. The only question to be decided before intending benefactors of science are urged to consider some such project is whether or not the facts likely to be won promise enough value to mankind.

An excellent case can be made out for answering yes. Dr. Shapley mentioned four chief lines of investigation suitable for such deep-mine laboratories: studies of gravity and of the variable length of the day, researches on the various kinds of earthquake waves, experiments on ether drift and tests of the biological effects of cosmic rays and of the rays from radium.

Astronomical theories indicate that the day ought to be growing slightly longer as the earth's rotation decreases a trifle from century to century because of friction from the tides. The actual length of the days seems, however, sometimes to be decreasing a tiny fraction of a second from year to year, as theory says that it should; sometimes to be increasing in a way for which no present theory provides. Observations underneath the earth, with a portion of the planet's crust and gravity overhead, might yield important clues to the cause of this mysterious wrong time kept by the terrestrial clock.

They were almost upon him when he leaped into action.

THE GRAY PLAGUE

By L. A. Eshbach

CHAPTER I

Five months before the beginning of that period of madness, that time of chaos and death that became known as the Gray Plague, the first of the strange meteors fell to Earth. It landed a few miles west of El Paso, Texas, on the morning of March 11th.

Maimed and captive, in the depths of an interplanetary meteor-craft, lay the only possible savior of plague-ridden Earth.

In a few hours a great throng of people gathered around the dully smoldering mass of fire-pitted rock, the upper half of which protruded from the Earth where it had buried itself, like a huge, roughly outlined hemisphere. And then, when the crowd had assumed its greatest proportions, the meteor, with a mighty, Earth-shaking roar, exploded.

A vast flood of radiance, more brilliant than the light of the sun, lit up the sky for miles around. One moment, a throng of curious people, a number of scientists, newspaper men—a crashing explosion—and then a great, yawning pit sending forth a blinding radiance! Destruction and death where life had been.

The brilliant light streamed from the pit for about ten minutes; then like a snuffed-out candle flame, it vanished.

The second of the strange meteors landed on the evening of March 13th, in the city of Peking, China. It demolished several buildings, and buried itself beneath the ruins. The Chinese, unaware of the tragedy at El Paso, gathered in the vicinity, and when the meteor exploded at about ten o'clock that night, were instantly destroyed. As in Texas, the great pit emitted a cloud of dazzling light for about ten minutes, throwing a brilliant glow over the city and its surroundings; then was extinguished.

The people of the world awoke to the fact that events worthy of more than passing interest were occurring. The press of every nation begin giving the strange meteors more and more publicity. Statements of different pseudo-scientists were published in explanation of the meteor's origin, statements that aroused world wide conjecture.

Approximately twenty-four hours after the falling of the second missile, the third one fell, landing near Madrid, Spain. The Spaniards, having received news of the El Paso and Peking tragedies, avoided the ugly mass of rock as though it were a dreaded pestilence. In every way its action was similar to that of its two predecessors.

The interest of the world was doubled now. The unusual similarity of the action of the meteors, and the regularity of their landings, seemed indicative of a definite, hostile purpose behind it all. A menace from the unknown—a peril from the skies!

Scientists began giving serious consideration to the unusual phenomenon, pottering around in the pits, wearing airs of puzzlement. But their investigations were of no avail, for nothing of any great significance came to light through their efforts.

At about that time, an announcement was made that created a furor. Astronomers in different parts of the United States reported that they had observed a bright flare of light leaping up from the darkened portion of the planet Venus. The astronomers had no definite idea of anything of importance in back of what they had seen; but not so the masses. The flare, they said, was caused by the release of another meteor!

From Venus! Missiles, hurled by Venerians, menacing the Earth! The silver planet became the subject of universal discussion; innumerable fantastic articles about it appeared in magazine sections of Sunday newspapers. And the astronomers of Earth turned their telescopes toward Venus with an interest they had never felt before.

Four days of expectant waiting passed by after the third meteor had fallen, while interest continued mounting at an accelerating pace. And then, at about two o'clock in the morning of the 18th, three great observatories, two in North America and one in England, recorded the falling of an extraordinarily large and unusually brilliant meteor that glowed with an intense, bluish-white light as it entered the Earth's atmosphere. And, unlike most meteors, this one was not consumed by its intense heat, but continued gleaming brilliantly until it vanished below the horizon. Simultaneous with the falling of the meteor, the Earth was rocked by one of the worst quakes in history.

Seismographs in all parts of the world recorded the tremors of the Earth, each indicating that the disturbance had occurred somewhere beneath the Atlantic ocean. Evidently the fourth meteor had fallen into the ocean, for the shaking of the Earth was obviously the result of the collision. That quakes had not followed the landing of the first three was due to the fact that they had been far smaller than the fourth.

And then, a short time after the earthquake, the worst storm in two hundred years broke over the Atlantic. Waves, mountain high, piled themselves upon each other in a wild frenzy; a shrieking wind lashed the waters into a liquid chaos. Great ocean-liners were tossed about like tiny chips; an appalling number of smaller ships were lost in that insane storm.

Nor was the destruction confined to the sea, for all along the Atlantic coast of North America and Europe, mighty walls of water rushed in, and wrecked entire towns and cities.

Fortunately the storm was of short duration; a few hours after it began, it subsided.

For a number of weeks public attention was centered upon the meteors and storm; but gradually, when nothing further occurred, the fickle interest of the masses began to wane. A month after the storm, the strange meteors were no longer mentioned by the press, and consequently, had passed from the public mind. Only the astronomers remembered, keeping their telescopes trained on Venus night after night.

Four months passed by during which nothing of an unusual nature came to the attention of the world. But at the end of that time, it suddenly dawned upon those nations whose shores touched the Atlantic ocean, that something extraordinary was happening. It was taking place so insidiously, so quietly, that it had attracted no great attention.

A series of inexplicable sea disasters had begun. Every ship that had traveled over a certain, regular steamship route, had disappeared, leaving no trace. Mysteriously, without warning, they had vanished; without a single S O S being sent, seven freighters had been lost. The disappearances had been called to the world's attention by the shipping companies, alarmed at the gradual loss of their boats.

Then other mysterious vanishings came to the attention of the world. Ships in all parts of the Atlantic were being lost. When this fact became known, trans-Atlantic commerce ceased almost over night. With the exception of a few privately owned yachts and freighters, the Atlantic became deserted.

And finally, a few days after the world became aware of the strange disappearances on the Atlantic, the Gray Plague introduced itself to humanity. Attempts were made to repress the facts: but the tragedy of the freighter, *Charleston*, in all its ghastliness and horror, became known in spite of all attempts at secrecy.

On the morning of August 3rd, the *Charleston* was found, half buried in the sand of a beach on the coast of Florida, cast there, evidently, by a passing storm. The freighter had been one of the first boats to disappear.

When the ship's discoverers boarded her, their eyes were greeted by a sight whose ghastliness filled them with a numbing horror. Indeed, so terrifying was the spectacle on the *Charleston*, that the discoverers, four boys of adolescent age, left in fear-stricken haste. Nor could they be induced to return to the ship's deck.

Later, a group of men from a nearby town boarded the freighter to investigate the boys' amazing report. In the group was a newspaper reporter who chanced to be in the vicinity on a minor story. It was through the reporter's account that the facts became known as quickly as they did.

When the men clambered up the side of the *Charleston* to her deck, they saw a spectacle the like of which had never before been seen on Earth. Although they had been prepared for the horror to some extent by the story of the boys, the sight on the *Charleston* exceeded their description to such a degree that, for the moment, the men were rendered speechless.

The deck of the *Charleston* was a shambles—a scene of sudden, chilling death. All about were strewn gray, lifeless bodies. Death had overtaken the crew in the midst of their duties, suddenly, without warning, it seemed. Bodies strewn about—yet nowhere was there sign of decay! Bodies, lifeless for days, or weeks—yet intact!

The men were fearfully impressed by the strangely grotesque positions of the corpses. With a few exceptions, they lay on the deck in abnormal, twisted masses of gray covered flesh. Somehow, they seemed flattened, as though they had been soft, jellylike, and had flowed, had settled, flat against the deck. Some were no more than three inches thick, and had spread out to such an extent that they looked like fantastic caricatures of human bodies. That unnatural change in their structure, and the ghastly, dead-gray color of their skins gave the corpses a horrifying, utterly repulsive appearance that made the flesh of the men crawl.

The bodies had a strangely soft aspect, as though they were still jellylike. One of the men, bolder than the rest, touched a body—and withdrew his hand in revulsion and surprise. For the ugly mass was cold, and as hard as bone: the tissues of the flesh seemingly replaced by a solid, bony substance. Later investigation revealed that all the dead on the *Charleston* had assumed a similar, bonelike solidity.

When the men left the freighter to report the tragedy to the proper authorities, their faces were blanched, and their nerves badly shaken. Yet their horror was nothing when compared with what it would have been, had they known what was to follow.

Rapidly the story of the *Charleston* spread. By means of the press, over the radio, even by word of mouth, the story of the horror on the freighter was given publicity. All over the United States and Canada it spread, and from thence to the rest of the world. Eagerly was the story accepted: here, at last, was the explanation of the sea disasters! And then, more than ever before, was the Atlantic ocean shunned.

The bodies of the seamen on the freighter were turned over to scientists for experimentation and research. It was thought that they might be able to discover the cause of the Gray Death, and with a knowledge of its cause, create something with which to free the Atlantic from its scourge.

The scientists' investigations only served to mystify the world to a greater degree. The only thing that came to light was the cause of the bodies' bonelike rigidity. In some inexplicable way the bones in the seamen had dissolved, and according to appearances, while the bodies were plastic, had flattened out. And then, strange and unnatural though it seemed, the calcium from the dissolved bones had gathered at the surface of each body, and combining with the flesh and skin, had formed the hard, bony shell that gave them their ghastly grayness, and their appearance of petrification. Aside from this, the scientists learned nothing; the cause of this amazing phenomenon was a complete mystery to them.

Slowly, methodically, step by step, the unusual had been taking place. From the time of the landing of the first strange meteor, up to the discovery of the *Charleston*, there had been a gradual increase in the significance of each succeeding event.

Then finally came the climax: the Gray Plague itself. All that preceded it faded into significance before the horror of the dread pestilence that seized the world with its destroying talons.

A short time after the discovery of the *Charleston*, the Plague made its first appearance on land. Slowly, pitilessly, inexorably, it began, taking its toll all along the Atlantic coast. From Newfoundland to Brazil; from the British Isles to Egypt, wherever people lived near the ocean, thousands were stricken with the dread malady.

The old and infirm were the most quickly affected; their weakened bodies could not withstand the ravage of the Plague as could those of younger people. An old man, walking along a large thoroughfare in Savannah, Georgia, suddenly uttered a fearful shriek and sank to the pavement. While the pedestrians watched with bulging eyes, he seemed to shrink, to flatten, to flow liquidly, turning a ghastly gray. Within an hour he was as hard as the men of the *Charleston*. Of all the millions, perhaps he was the first.

Others followed in the wake of the first victim, young as well as old; three hours after the death in Savannah, every channel of communication was choked with news of a constantly increasing number of casualties. A Boston minister, preaching a funeral sermon, collapsing beside the coffin; a lineman on a telegraph pole, overcome, falling—and splashing! A thousand incongruous tragedies shocking humanity.

In Europe the action of the Plague was the same as in North America. Death stalking the sea-coast, destroying thousands; ignorant fishermen, men of learning, women and children of every age—all were grist to be ground in the mill of the Gray Plague.

Before a week had gone by, no one remained alive in the villages, towns and cities all along the Atlantic. New York, London, all the large coast cities were deserted by the living, left to the rigid dead. From the largest metropolis to the smallest hamlet, all became body-glutted tombs.

And then, on the morning of October 12th, news was given to the world that threw mankind into a panic. The Plague was moving inland! Slowly, yet relentlessly it spread, no longer confining its effect to the sea-coast, but moving farther and farther inland toward the heart of the two continents, driving mankind before it. For people fled in insane terror before the advancing death. Nor was there escape from the menace—no antidote to counteract, no sanctuary wherein to hide.

To North and South, to East and West, the pestilence spread, destroying as it went. Unless there were some miraculous intervention, the human race would be destroyed!

Officials of the world were at their wits' end; scientists threw up their hands in despair. The Plague was an insoluble puzzle—enigmatical, utterly inexplicable, beyond the knowledge of Earth.

Scientists and doctors were brutally slain during that period by fear-crazed mobs, because of their inability to rescue the world from the grip of the Plague. Thousands of people died while striving to escape from the Gray Death, crushed by passing motor vehicles, or starving in the congested areas. Gone was the boasted civilization of man—humanity sinking rapidly to the level of the beast; gone, destroyed in a few weeks!

And then one day when the end seemed perilously close, there was ushered into the presence of the remnant of the United States officials who had gathered in San Francisco, a twisted monstrosity of a man, fearfully scarred and deformed. He was closeted with them for two hours. At the end of that time an excited official communicated with the leader of the American scientists.

"A cure for the Plague has been discovered!" he cried in joyful tones. "Man still has a chance!"

Before an hour had passed by, scientists were in possession of cultures of germs that would destroy the bacilli of the Gray Death. The hope of salvation restored some semblance of order; and in a very short time the development of the germs was going forward as rapidly as skilled bacteriologists could carry it. Forces of doctors were marshalled to administer the cure, inoculating all who were untouched by the Plague.

At about that time, a small, bronze-colored sphere arose into the air above San Francisco, and sped eastward with amazing velocity. It flashed over the United States, over the Atlantic ocean, and over western Europe, finally landing in the midst of the European hordes. There its operator, a deformed cripple, left bacteria similar to those he had given to the United States.

In a short time Europe, too, was busily engaged in developing the bacteria, and inoculating her people.

Many others died before the world was rendered immune, but at last mankind let its labors cease. The Gray Plague was overcome.

Then the work of reclaiming the deserted areas was begun; then, too, was started the ghastly task of disposing of the countless, rigid dead. And finally, a great steamer left New York harbor, and started across the Atlantic. It was the purpose of the men on board to destroy utterly the source of the Plague.

But long before that occurred, humanity had heard the story of Phillip Parkinson, the man who saved the world—had heard, and had honored the deliverer of mankind.

Parkinson's story follows:

CHAPTER II

The steam yacht, Diana, bound for the Azores and points south, was two days out from Miami when the great meteor fell into the Atlantic. On the after deck, leaning over the rail, watching the moonlit waters, stood Phillip Parkinson, owner of the yacht. A bacteriologist of international fame was Parkinson, on an early vacation to recuperate from the effects of a strenuous winter of research. Nervous, rather high-strung, he had been unable to sleep; at about one in the morning of the 18th of March, he had come up on deck.

He had stood there for about an hour when suddenly there appeared in the sky above him, a meteor, a great disc of blue-white incandescence. It seemed to be rushing straight down toward him; instinctively he leaped back, as though to avoid the fiery missile.

As the constantly expanding disc flashed through the hundred miles of Earth's atmosphere, the ocean, as far as eye could see, became as light as day. Bathed in that baleful, white glare, Parkinson, bewildered, dazed, half-blinded, watched the approaching stellar visitant.

In a few moments it struck—no more than two miles away. In the last, bright flare of blue-white light, Parkinson saw a gigantic column of steam and boiling water leap up from the sea. Then thick, impenetrable darkness fell—darkness that was intensified by its contrast with the meteor's blinding light.

For ten tense, breathless seconds utter silence hung over the sea ... then, for those on the yacht, the world went mad! A shrill, unearthly shriek—the sound of the meteor's passage through the atmosphere; an ear-splitting roar, as of the simultaneous release of the thunder-drums of ages; a howling demon of wind; a solid wall of raging, swirling water of immeasurable height—all united in an indescribable chaos that bewildered those on board the Diana, and that lifted the yacht and—threw it upon its side!

When the first rushing mountain of lathering, thundering water crashed upon the yacht, Parkinson felt himself hurtling through the roaring air. For a moment he heard the infernal pandemonium of noise ... then the strangling, irresistible brine closed over his head.

A blackness deeper than that of the night—and Parkinson knew no more....

Slowly consciousness returned to the bacteriologist. It came under the guise of a dull, yet penetrating throbbing coming from beneath the surface on which he lay. Vaguely he wondered at it; he had not yet entirely cast off the enshrouding stupor that gripped him.

Gradually he came into full possession of his faculties—and became aware of a dull aching throughout his entire body. In his chest it seemed to be intensified; every breath caused a sharp pang of pain.

Faltering and uncertain, he arose and peered around. Before, lay the open sea, calm now, and peaceful. Long, rolling swell swept in and dashed themselves against the rocks a few feet away. Rocks? For a moment Parkinson stared at the irregular shore-line in dazed wonder. Then as his mind cleared, the strangeness of his position flashed upon him.

Solid earth was under his feet! Although he must be hundreds of miles from shore, in some way he had drifted upon land. So far as he knew, there were no islands in that part of the Atlantic; yet his very position belied the truth.

He could not have drifted to the mainland; the fact that he was alive precluded all possibilities of that, for he would have drowned in far less time than the latter thought implied.

He turned and inspected the land upon which he had been cast. A small, barren island, bleak and inhospitable, and strangely metallic, met his gaze. The rays of the sun beating down upon it were thrown back with an uncomfortable intensity; the substance of the island was a lustrous, copperlike metal. No soil softened the harshness of the surface; indescribably rugged and pitted was the two hundred-foot expanse. It reminded Parkinson of a bronze relief-map of the moon.

For a moment he puzzled over the strangeness of the unnatural island; then suddenly he realized the truth. This was the meteor! Obviously, this was the upper side of the great sphere from space, protruding above the sea.

Fortunate for him that the meteor had not been completely covered by water, he thought—but was it fortunate? True, he was alive now, thanks to the tiny island, but how long would he remain alive without food or water, and without hope of securing either? Unless he would be picked up by a passing steamer, he would die a far more unpleasant death than that of drowning. Some miracle had saved him from a watery grave; it would require another to rescue him from a worse fate.

Even now he was beginning to feel thirsty. He had no way of determining how long he had been unconscious, but that it was at least ten hours, he was certain, for the sun had been at its zenith when he had awakened. No less than fifteen hours had gone by since water—other than that of the sea—had passed his lips. And the fact that it was impossible for him to quench his thirst only served to render it more acute.

In order to take his mind from thoughts of his thirst and of the immediate future, he rapidly circled the island. As he had expected, it was utterly barren. With shoulders drooping in despair he settled wearily to a seat on the jagged mass of metal high up on top of the meteor.

An expression of sudden interest lit up his face. For a second time he felt that particular throbbing, that strange pulsing beneath the surface of the meteor. But now it was far more noticeable than before. It seemed to be directly below him, and very close to the surface.

Parkinson could not tell how long he sat there, but from the appearance of the sun, he thought that at the very shortest, an hour passed by while he remained on that spot. And during that time, the throbbing gradually increased until the metal began vibrating under his feet.

Suddenly the bacteriologist leaped aside. The vibrating had reached its height, and the meteor seemed to lurch, to tilt at a sharp angle. His leap carried him to firm footing again. And then, his thirst and hopeless position completely forgotten, Parkinson stared in fascination at the amazing spectacle before him.

An eighteen-foot disc of metal, a perfect circle, seemed to have been cut out of the top of the meteor. While he watched, it began turning slowly, ponderously, and started sinking into the meteor. As it sank, Parkinson fancied that it grew transparent, and gradually vanished into nothingness—but he wasn't sure.

A great pit, eighteen feet wide, but far deeper, lay before him in the very place where, not more than ten minutes before, he had stood. Not a moment too soon had he leaped.

Motionless he stood there, waiting in tense expectation. What would happen next, he had not the least idea, but he couldn't prevent his imagination from running riot.

He hadn't long to wait before his watching was rewarded. A few minutes after the pit appeared, he heard a loud, high-pitched whir coming from the heart of the meteor. As it grew louder, it assumed a higher and still higher key, finally rising above the range of human ears. And at that moment the strange vehicle arose to the surface.

A simple-appearing mechanism was the car, consisting of a twelve-foot sphere of the same bronze-like metal that made up the meteor, with a huge wheel, like a bronze cincture, around its middle. It was the whirling of this great wheel that had caused the high-pitched whirring. The entire, strange machine was surrounded by a peculiar green radiance, a radiance that seemed to crackle ominously as the sphere hovered over the mouth of the pit.

For a moment the car hung motionless, then it drifted slowly to the surface of the meteor, landing a few feet away from Parkinson. Hastily he drew back from the greenly phosphorescent thing—but not before he had experienced an unpleasant prickling sensation over his entire body.

As the bacteriologist drew away, there was a sharp, audible click within the interior of the sphere; and the green radiance vanished. At the same moment, three heavy metal supports sprang from equi-distant points in the sides of the car, and held the sphere in a balanced position on the rounded top of the meteor.

There was a soft, grating sound on the opposite side of the car. Quickly, Parkinson circled it—and stopped short in surprise.

Men were descending from an opening in the side of the sphere! Parkinson had reasoned that since the meteor had come from the depths of space, any being in its interior, unnatural as that seemed, would have assumed a form quite different from the human. Of course, conditions on Earth could be approximated on another planet. At any rate, whatever the explanation, the sphere was emitting men!

They were men—but there was something queer about them. They were very tall—seven feet or more—and very thin; and their skins were a delicate, transparent white. They looked rather ghostly in their tight-fitting white suits. It was not this that made them seem queer, however: it was an indefinite something, a vague suggestion of heartless inhumanity, of unearthliness, that was somehow repulsive and loathsome.

There were three of them, all very similar in appearance and bearing. Their surprise at the sight of Parkinson, if anything, was greater than the start their appearance had given him. He, at least, had expected to see beings of some sort, while the three had been taken completely by surprise.

For a moment they surveyed him with staring, cold-blue eyes. Then Parkinson extended his hand, and as cordially as he could, exclaimed:

"Hello! Welcome to Earth!"

The visitors from space ignored his advances and continued staring at him. Their attitude at first was quizzical, speculative, but slowly a hostile expression crept into their eyes.

Suddenly, with what seemed like common consent, they faced each other, and conversed in low tones in some unintelligible tongue. For almost a minute they talked, while Parkinson watched them in growing apprehension.

Finally they seemed to have reached some definite conclusion; with one accord they turned and moved slowly toward the bacteriologist, something distinctly menacing in their attitudes. The men from the meteor were tall, but they were thin; Parkinson, too, was large, and his six-foot length was covered with layers of solid muscle. As the three advanced toward him, he doubled his fists, and crouched in readiness for the expected attack.

They were almost upon him when he leaped into action. A crushing left to his stomach sent the first one to the meteor-top, where he lay doubled up in pain. But that was the only blow that Parkinson struck; in a moment he found himself lying prone upon his back, utterly helpless, his body completely paralyzed. What they had done to him, he did not know; all that he could remember was two thin bodies twining themselves around him—a sharp twinge of pain at the base of his skull; then absolute helplessness.

One of the tall beings grasped Parkinson about the waist, and with surprising strength, threw him over his shoulder. The other assisted his groaning fellow. When the latter had recovered to some extent, the three ascended the ladder that led into the metal sphere.

The interior of the strange vehicle, as far as Parkinson could see, was as simple as its exterior. There was no intricate machinery of any sort in the square room; probably what machinery there was lay between the interior and exterior walls of the sphere. As for controls, these consisted of several hundred little buttons that studded one of the walls.

When they entered the vehicle, Parkinson was literally, and none too gently, dumped upon the floor. The man who had carried him stepped over to the controls. Like those of a skilled typist, his long, thin fingers darted over the buttons. In a moment the sphere was in motion.

There were no more thrills for Parkinson in that ride than he would have derived from a similar ride in an elevator. They sank very slowly for some minutes, it seemed to him; then they stopped with a barely noticeable jar.

The door of the car was thrust aside by one of the three, and Parkinson was borne from the sphere. A bright, coppery light flooded the interior of the meteor, seeming to radiate from its walls. In his helpless state, and in the awkward position in which he was carried, with his head close to the floor, he could see little of the room through which they passed, in spite of the light. Later, however, he learned that it was circular in shape, and about twice the diameter of the cylindrical tube that led into it. The wall that bound this chamber was broken at regular intervals by tall, narrow, doorways, each leading into a different room.

Parkinson was carried into one of these, and was placed in a high-backed metal chair. After he had been strapped fast, one of the men placed his hands at the base of the bacteriologist's skull; he felt a sudden twinge of pain; and his strange paralysis left him suddenly.

---

e knew it was useless to struggle; without resisting, he let them place upon his head a cap-like device that seemed lost in a tangled maze of machinery. Each meteor-man grasped one of the instruments resembling old-time radio head-phones that were fastened to Parkinson's head-gear, and clamped it over his ears.

The bacteriologist heard a steady, humming drone, like a swarm of angry bees—felt a peculiar, soothing warmth about his head; and then he slept.

Only a moment or two seemed to have passed when he awoke. The strange device on his head was removed and put away; and then, to Parkinson's amazement, one of the three men, evidently the leader, spoke—in English!

"Now that you have recovered consciousness," he remarked in a cold, expressionless voice, "you had better realize at the very beginning that you are completely in our power. Any effort to escape will be futile, for there is only one way to reach the outside; the opening through the top; and only one means of travel through that opening: the sphere. And since you know nothing about the operation of the machine, any attempt to run it would be disastrous to you.

"If you promise to refrain from violence, we'll release you, and give you some measure of freedom. We'll do this because you can be of assistance to us in one of our tasks here on your planet."

Parkinson assented readily; he knew he could gain nothing by rejecting their offer. "Of course I'll promise. But—but, how did you learn English?" he asked in bewilderment.

"You taught us," the leader replied. "That device we placed upon your head created a duplicate of your knowledge in our minds. We knew your language, your world, indeed, yourself, as well as you do."

Parkinson shook his head in amazement. Another question came to his mind as the men released him. He was interrupted before he could give it expression.

“Don't ask," the leader exclaimed. "I'll tell our entire story so that you'll have no occasion to annoy us with your questions.

"We're Venerians," he began, "inhabitants of the planet you call Venus. For ages our world has been overcrowded. A short time ago, the conditions became so acute that something had to be done. It was suggested that we seek another habitable planet to which our people could migrate.

"Your Earth was thought to be the world with physical conditions most closely resembling those of Acor, or Venus. Our scientists set to work immediately, using forces and devices with which you are totally unfamiliar, and constructed several missiles which they hurled at Earth. These missiles, spherical masses closely resembling meteors, were set to explode after a certain period of contact with an atmosphere similar to our own. By their explosion we on Venus could determine whether or not this world had a breathable atmosphere.

"Upon our deciding that the Earth was habitable, we built this great machine. It is chiefly composed of our greatest heat-resister, a metal we call thoque; I see no corresponding word in your vocabulary; evidently you are unfamiliar with the element, or else it is unknown on Earth.

"After our flight through space, automatically controlled, by the way, on Venus, we landed here. With our thoque disintegrator, we bored a passageway to the surface of this great sphere. Then we entered the car, rose to the top of the passageway, and discovered you.

"That is a brief synopsis of our actions—and it must suffice! Ask no questions; we do not wish to be disturbed by the blind gropings of your primitive mind!"

There was a cold finality in the Venerian's voice that convinced Parkinson that for the moment, at least, he had better forget the many questions that had surged up in his mind.

The Venerian leader spoke again. "From our observations of your mind, we know that you have not had food or water for a rather lengthy period of time. It is not our purpose to starve you: you shall eat and drink."

A minute later Parkinson sat at a very high table in one of the rooms, drinking water from Venus, and eating the fare of an alien world.

Days passed by, merging into weeks, while Parkinson lost all track of time. The bacteriologist's existence became a ceaseless round of toil. The Venerian had said that he would be given some measure of freedom, because he would be of use to them; he had not been with them long ere he learned what that use was.

One of the rooms was filled with great slabs of thoque; it was Parkinson's task to carry the slabs to the vehicle at the base of the shaft, one by one; to rise to the surface with them, accompanied by two of the men—the third was working on the surface—and there unload them. Day after day this continued.

Hope of escaping was almost dead in Parkinson's breast, because he was constantly under the surveillance of those hard, blue eyes. Only one thing kept hope alive: by watching the Venerians operate the car, he was slowly gaining a knowledge of the meaning of the many buttons in the wall. Some day, if an opportunity came, he meant to be ready to take advantage of it.

Once, shortly after his monotonous toil began, Parkinson experienced a great flare of hope for deliverance. They had just brought another slab to the surface, when a steamer appeared above the horizon. It was far away, but its crew must surely have seen the island.

But his expectations were short-lived. One of the three drew from beneath his tight-fitting, white garments a little, metal object, a long tube, with a handle at one end, and pointed it at the vessel. For a moment he held it thus, moving it slowly backward and forward: then he returned it to its place of concealment, and turned away with an air of indifference. And Parkinson saw the ship burst suddenly into flame, a few minutes later to sink beneath the waves.

Shaken to the depths of his being, Parkinson resumed his work. The inhumanity of these saturnine Venerians filled him with a dread so great that he refused to admit it to himself. That that had not been the first time that they had destroyed a ship, he felt sure; his heart sank, and grew more hopeless.

At last his task of carrying slabs was finished. The room was empty, and the work completed. A great tower, entirely covering the island, reared its head into the sky. In appearance, it resembled a very tall lighthouse. This resemblance held true only until its top was reached; there it ended. From the tower's top extended four long, hollow arms, so constructed that they whirled about the tower at a mad pace when the machinery with which they were connected was started. In addition, arrangement was made for a powerful blast of air to be sent through the tubes when the Venerians so desired.

What the purpose of this great edifice was, Parkinson could not guess: later, he learned the horrible significance of it all.

After the tower was finished, the bacteriologist was left to his own devices to a great extent, though always closely watched by one of his captors. They let him eat all the food he desired, and let him lie around as much as he wished, regaining his health and strength. This was a pleasant surprise for him: he took full advantage of his privileges.

Then, one day when Parkinson had fully recovered from the effects of his grueling labors, the leader of the Venerians approached him from behind, and before he could raise a hand in defense, had rendered him helplessly paralyzed.

"You will now be given a second opportunity to help the cause of Venus on Earth," he said in his expressionless voice. And so saying, he lifted Parkinson, and bore him into one of the rooms.

CHAPTER III

At no time while he was held captive by the Venerians was Parkinson as hopeless, or as completely filled with despair as when he was carried into this room. There was something depressing about the chamber, something that gripped his heart with the chill hand of dread. He had a feeling of impending evil.

The few momentary glimpses of the chamber that he had gotten while he was being carried, sufficed to convince Parkinson that this was a laboratory, or—he shuddered at the thought—an operating room. The walls, floor and ceiling were composed of a white porcelainlike substance: from these walls, strangely, streamed the same coppery light that filled the entire meteor.

Entirely concealing one wall was a long, glass case, constructed to form countless little niches, each of which held a small, transparent vessel. At the back of the room was a high table, covered with transparent cases which were filled with complex instruments of every description, some similar to those on Earth; others entirely different.

The thing that brought the thought of an operating room to Parkinson's mind was the long, white slab that rested on metal uprights in the room's center—an operating table. A moment after they entered the room, he had his theory substantiated: the Venerian leader placed him on the white slab, stretching him to full length. It was an operating table—and he was to be the subject of their operation!

He had lain there but a moment when two of the Venerians approached, one on either side, and began removing his clothing. It was not long before he lay on the cold slab, entirely nude.

While he was being stripped, he heard the leader of the Venerians moving about, heard the click of glass, the rasp of metal upon metal. But, unable to move his eyes, he had seen none of his activities, except to note that several of the little vessels had been taken from their resting places.

When the two had finished disrobing him, and had replaced him upon his back, the leader appeared. He looked down at Parkinson, a queer expression in his hard, blue eyes. He seemed to hesitate a moment: then he spoke.

"Earthling," he said in his toneless voice, "I have decided to tell you of our intentions. You are going to play a very important part in our scheme, and it is only fitting that you should know. You can do nothing to hinder our plans: you are giving us incalculable aid: and it affords me some degree of satisfaction to tell you this.

"As you know, Earthling, we purpose to have the people of Acor to come to Earth to live, to relieve the congested conditions of our own world. Obviously, there is no room for two types of intelligent beings on one planet—your race must go! It is our intention to destroy all human life on Earth!

"We intend accomplishing this with Venerian microbes. From the record of your knowledge, I've learned that diseases of various kinds are common on Earth. We expected that such would be the case, and thus, you would not be immune to germs, so we came prepared. Each of the small compartments in that case that you may have seen, contains a culture of a different germ. After we have determined which Venerian bacilli will be the most effective, we will develop them in great quantities, and loose them upon your world.

"In the selecting process, you will play your part. Since our germs may have a different effect upon your bodies than they do upon Venerians, we will inoculate you with different diseases, and watch their effects upon you.

"Of course, you yourself will be in no great danger, for we will have the diseases under our constant control. On Acor we have abolished disease entirely, having a reagent or an antitoxin for every malady; we will use our cures upon you immediately after we have seen how you react to each disease.

"What we desire is a bacillus that will take effect when it is breathed in through the lungs. If the disease is of such a nature as to instill fear in the minds of observers, so much the better; but that is unnecessary. When we discover a microbe of that nature, we will be ready to act.

"By the way, our work has been lessened to a great degree by the fact that you are a bacteriologist. The knowledge we gain from you has enabled us to eliminate at least half of our microbes. All Venerian germs that are duplicated on Earth will be left out of our calculations. Only those unknown to your planet will be tried upon you."

When the Venerian had finished his explanation, each word of which had sounded like a death knell to Parkinson, the bacteriologist lay on the slab in the grip of a nightmare of horror. The cold-blooded brutality of these Venerian beasts, and the thought of lying there helpless with his body the prey of unknown diseases, filled him with a maddening fear and dread.

Mightily he struggled to break the uncanny bonds that held him paralyzed, but it was of no avail. His body retained its helpless rigidity.

Only for a moment was Parkinson left to his fearful musings; then the Venerians begin their work. A tall table on wheels was brought from somewhere, and drawn to the side of the slab. Upon this various instruments were placed, side by side with numerous flat vessels containing germ cultures. Parkinson saw none of this, but from the sounds that came to his ears he could infer what was taking place.

Finally, everything seemed to be in readiness. The Venerian leader bent over Parkinson for a moment: and the latter felt a sharp pain in his side. Then the Venerian withdrew.

Slowly, interminably, the time dragged by while the microbes that had been introduced into his body were at their work. How long he lay there with the Venerians watching, he could not tell, but it seemed to be hours. During that time he felt himself gripped by an increasingly violent fever. Unbearable heat flooded his body. And because of his helplessness, he could do nothing to relieve his pain and discomfort. It was maddening!

When he thought he had reached the limit of his endurance, and felt that he would go insane in another moment, the Venerian leader injected something into his side. He became aware of an immediate sense of relief; in an unbelievably short time the fever had left him and he was himself again.

There followed for Parkinson hours of nightmare agony, while the Venerians experimented with his living body. Time after time he was inoculated with strange bacilli that wracked him with tortures indescribable. Hideous diseases covered him with festering sores; twisted his flesh into a repellent mass of scars; left him weakened and deformed. Had it not been for the incredible curative powers of the Venerians, he would have died then; but always, when the end seemed at hand, they brought him back to life, only to subject him to other horrors.

After what seemed countless ages, the Venerians left him alone. Under the powerful effects of their cures, Parkinson began to recover. Hope welled up in his heart; perhaps the terrible experiments were ended.

When he was almost certain that the torture was over, his hopes were suddenly destroyed. The three Venerians approached again, each bearing a number of vessels containing germ cultures. These they placed on the table at Parkinson's side; then two of them withdrew, leaving the leader to continue his work. Uttering a few words in the Venerian tongue, he occupied himself with something on the table, and a moment later turned toward the bacteriologist, a long needle in his hands.

Parkinson felt a great burning pain in his left arm, as though a searing, hot needle had been thrust into his flesh. In a moment this vanished. Then a feeling of irresistible lassitude overwhelmed him; an unbearable weariness filled him with longing for rest, peace—death. This, too, was of short duration.

With the passing of the weariness, Parkinson became aware of a sharp throbbing in his arm. Rapidly this increased in violence, until suddenly an unbearable, excruciating agony seized him. Far greater was this than any pain he had suffered before. For a moment he struggled to scream, to move, to do anything to relieve his agony. There seemed to be a sudden snap—a cry of anguish burst from his lips—and his senses left him. Just as the bonds of paralysis had broken, he had lost consciousness.

Life returned to Parkinson very slowly. In a daze he stared around, uncomprehending. Then suddenly he realized that he was no longer paralyzed: nor was he in the operating room. The bed on which he lay was soft, comfortable; the room, unfamiliar. But not for long did his mind dwell upon this; in a few moments his eyelids closed, and he slept the sleep of complete mental and physical exhaustion.

Daring the weeks that followed, Parkinson did little other than sleep. Occasionally he arose, either to stretch himself, or to secure food, but for the greater part of the time he remained in bed. His body was a mere shadow of its former self as the result of his terrible experience on the white slab: his incessant sleeping, necessary because of his weakened condition, served to bring him back to his former health. The Venerians seemed glad to have it thus: asleep, he did not disturb their activities.

When he had awakened from his first period of natural slumber, he had received a terrible shock. His left arm was gone, amputated at the shoulder. Strangely, the wound had healed while he slept, probably the result of the Venerian doctoring, so there was no pain: but the shock had been terrible.

After he had recovered from the effects of that shock, he had resolved to make the Venerians pay for what they had done. And then he had realized that the inhuman brutes must be destroyed for a greater reason: unless he interfered, he believed that they would carry out their intention of destroying all human life.

As the weeks passed by, while strength was returning to Parkinson, he learned in a general way what the invaders were doing. They were engaged in developing vast quantities of microbes to be spread over Earth. When these were ready, a great amount of fine dust that the Venerians had brought with them, was impregnated with the bacilli. This was then taken up into the tower, where, as Parkinson learned later, it was blown out through the four tubes that spun around the tower's top, to drift through the air—to enter human bodies—to destroy life.

The Venerians worked with the cultures and impregnated dust without protection of any sort: evidently they were immune to the disease. Later Parkinson learned that he was likewise immune; they had rendered him so after trying the germs upon him.

Gradually the bacteriologist's health returned—so gradually that his captors seemed not to notice it. He was glad of this, for their vigilance had relaxed, and he did not want it renewed. Even when he was as strong and well as ever, he spent much time in bed, shamming illness. And when he could do so without danger of detection, he kept a close watch upon the three, waiting for a time when he would be entirely alone.

At last his opportunity came. The three Venerians rose to the surface together, leaving him in his room, to all outward appearances, asleep. But sleep was far from him at that moment; he had been watching.

Shortly after the sphere had vanished up the shaft, Parkinson emerged from his room. For a moment he surveyed the circle of doors: then he shrugged his shoulders. They all looked alike to him. Quickly he crossed the room, and pressed a button that mechanically opened a door. It was his purpose, first of all, to secure a weapon; one room would do as well as another for a beginning.

At first glance Parkinson was struck by the strange familiarity of this chamber: then, after a moment, he recognized it. A tall, high-backed metal chair in its center was its mark of identification. This was the chamber wherein the Venerians had transferred a record of his knowledge to their minds.

Carefully he looked around in search of a weapon, but the room held nothing but the chair and the thought transference device. In a moment he withdrew, closing the door behind him.

In the next room he entered, he was fortunate. This chamber was filled with strange devices of various kinds. While curiously inspecting the intricate machines, he saw something that brought a smile of satisfaction to his lips.

Against one wall stood a tall, glass case, one of the shelves of which held several metal devices that Parkinson immediately recognized as being the

Venerians' weapons. Poignantly he remembered how a similar device had destroyed a ship.

Leaving the door slightly ajar, he crossed to the case and secured one of the weapons. For a moment he studied it. There was nothing complex about the mechanism; a cursory examination sufficed to reveal how it was operated. Pressure on a little knob at the back of the handle released the devastating ray.

He was about to slip the device into his pocket when he stiffened involuntarily. There was a sound of movement outside the room—he heard a step on the metal floor—then he whirled.

One of the Venerians stood in the doorway, a menacing frown on his face. He was crouching, ready to spring upon Parkinson.

Quick as thought, the bacteriologist leveled his newly-acquired weapon, and pressed on the knob. There was a sudden spurt of flame from the Venerian's body; then it crumpled, sagging, shrinking together.

Hastily Parkinson released the pressure on the little knob, aghast at the destructive power of his little weapon. Then, as he remembered the torture he had endured at their hands, he directed the ray upon the ashes, until they, too, were consumed, leaving naught but a dark patch on the floor.

For several minutes Parkinson stood there in deep thought. There was no immediate danger from the two remaining Venerians, for they were up in the tower, while the sphere was in the meteor; so he could think with utmost safety. Deep thought and careful planning were necessary now, for he had taken the step that must mean either his death or the death of the Venerians.

Suddenly he leaped into action; he had decided upon his next move. Crossing to the case he secured another weapon. He wasn't sure that they could be effectively discharged without re-loading; handicapped as he was with one arm gone, he had to be certain of the reliability of his means of defense. Then he left the room, and crossed to the huge thoque sphere.

It was the work of a moment to enter this, and prepare to ascend. This done, he turned his attention to the numerous knobs on the wall. He had not seen them for quite a while; it was with difficulty that he recalled which knobs controlled the car's ascent. At last, hesitantly, but correctly, he pressed on the knobs, and the sphere rose slowly toward the surface.

At the proper moment, Parkinson, brought the vehicle to a halt, and slid back the door. Furtively he peered around. The Venerians were on the other side of the tower. Quickly he lowered the ladder and descended.

As he stepped to the floor, a sudden cry of dismay fell upon his ears. One of the Venerians, coming around the car, had discovered him. Without a moment's hesitation, Parkinson aimed his little weapon, and pressed upon the knob. Like his fellow, the Venerian fell to the floor, a heap of charred ashes.

With the second Venerian destroyed, Parkinson dashed around the sphere, metal cylinder held in readiness. The leader of the Venerians was stealing stealthily around the other side of the car, his hand fumbling beneath his garment.

"Stop!" Parkinson cried. "Raise your hands above your head—empty!" A cylinder clattered to the metal floor as the Venerian's hands moved skyward.

"Keep your back turned!" Parkinson snapped as the invader began about. "I won't hesitate to press on this little knob, at your first hostile move! I'd thoroughly enjoy burning you to a crisp, so be very careful."

While talking, Parkinson had moved slowly toward the man from Venus; now, almost upon him, he quickly dropped his weapon into a pocket, and swung a terrible blow at the base of his skull. The Venerian fell to the floor without a groan, unconscious.

Parkinson stared at the recumbent figure rather dubiously for a moment. If only he had his other arm! But it was gone; with an impatient shake of his head he stooped and raised the senseless invader.

It was anything but an easy task for the bacteriologist to carry his seven-foot burden up the ladder and into the sphere, but finally, he succeeded in doing so. Then, without delay, he lowered the car into the meteor again.

As he bore the Venerian from the vehicle, he tried to decide upon his next move. Obviously, he had to secure the one surviving invader, so that he would not be a menace to Parkinson when he revived. And then the logical thing to do would be, in some way, to secure information from him as to how to cure the disease that was spreading over the world.

The logical thing to do, yes—but how? With only one arm, the simple task of binding the Venerian presented considerable difficulty. How much more difficult would it be to force anything from him?

Then the solution of the first problem presented itself to Parkinson. What was to prevent his strapping this being into the high-backed chair to which he had been secured some time before? Quickly he crossed the circular room to the door he had first passed through while searching for a weapon.

Ten minutes later, when the Venerian regained his senses, he was fastened securely to the tall, metal chair.

"Well," Parkinson addressed him, "conditions seem to be reversed now, and you're the underdog. I've nipped your invasion in the bud. All your elaborate preparations are wasted."

Something resembling a sneer wreathed the Venerian's thin lips; a mocking gleam lit his cold, blue eyes.

"So our efforts have been wasted, have they? I'm afraid I can't agree with you. Already, enough bacteria have been released to destroy all life, though it will take longer than we desire. Even though you kill me, our goal will still be reached. The human race will die!"

A cloud of gloom fell upon Parkinson. He had expected this; but he had been hoping that he was wrong.

"Then there's only one thing for me to do, and that is: I'll have to force you to tell me how to undo the damage you've done."

The Venerian smiled mirthlessly. "You have absolutely no chance of accomplishing that," he said. "We've done our work too well to allow any interference now.

"You do not know this, but we have released upon your world the worst malady ever known to Venus. There is only one remedy; and I'm the only one who knows it, or who has the means wherewith to accomplish it. And I certainly won't tell!"

The worried expression on Parkinson's face increased in intensity. There was something in the Venerian's voice that convinced him that he meant what he said.

Then suddenly his countenance cleared, and a happy smile replaced his frown.

"Perhaps you won't tell, but I think you will. There are more ways than one of forcing you."

Parkinson had hit upon a solution to his problem. The Venerians had reproduced his knowledge in their brains; why wouldn't it be possible for him to reverse the operation?

In a moment he secured the thought-transference apparatus from a case in the rear of the room, and bore it to the chair, and in spite of the Venerian leader's struggles, placed it upon his head. He put the head-phones over his own ears, and began fumbling with the controls.

Suddenly he seemed to strike the right combination. There was a faint, humming drone in his ears; after a moment this was replaced by a loud crackling—and the knowledge of the man from Venus was becoming his own.

Somewhat dazed, Parkinson shut off the current. His mind was in a turmoil. He was in possession of knowledge of such an amazing character that, for the moment he had lost his mental equilibrium. Indeed, so strange was his new-found knowledge, that he could not grasp the significance of even half of the facts in his mind.

But already, he knew how, with animal electricity, they had paralyzed him; knew what had happened to him on the operating table; knew the nature of the dread disease that destroyed his arm; the Gray Plague—and knew the cure!

A sudden thought arrested this review of his new knowledge. The Gray Plague! At that very moment incalculable quantities of the deadly bacilli were being cast into the air. And he was doing nothing about it!

He glanced at the Venerian. He was still unconscious, and would remain so for some minutes to come. And even if he did recover his senses, he was securely fastened to the chair; Parkinson dashed out of the room, crossed to the sphere, and passed through the open doorway.

Without hesitation he manipulated the controls, directed by his Venerian knowledge. Rapidly the sphere rose to the surface.

As it came to rest on the floor of the tower, Parkinson sprang from the car, and headed toward a mass of intricate machinery that filled fully a quarter of the great building.

Even this caused him no great concern; he was as familiar with it as he would have been had he constructed it. For some moments he was busy with numerous dials and levers; then the release of the germs was stopped.

Parkinson spent several minutes in examining the contents of the tower, his Earthly mind lost in wonder at the strange things his Venerian knowledge revealed to him. Then he entered the sphere again, and sank into the meteor.

As he moved toward the room that held the Venerian, his mind was busy with conjectures as to what he would do with his prisoner. It was necessary for the bacteriologist to reach the mainland as quickly as possible, and make use of his knowledge of the cure for the Gray Plague. He didn't want to kill the man; he couldn't free him; yet if he left him strapped to the chair, he'd surely die of starvation.

Still undecided, he thrust open the door. With a startled gasp he stopped short. Somehow the Venerian had freed himself; at that moment he leaped toward Parkinson.

Instinctively the bacteriologist flung up his hand in a defensive attitude. The onrushing Venerian caught Parkinson's out-thrust fist in the pit of his stomach, and doubled up in pain. While he was thus defenseless, Parkinson placed a well-directed blow on the side of the Venerian's jaw, a blow carrying every ounce of his strength.

So great was the force of the punch, that it lifted the man from Venus and cast him headlong upon the floor. His head landed with a sickening thud. Unmoving, he lay where he had fallen.

Parkinson knelt over him for a moment, then arose. Without question, the man was dead. The Venerian had solved the bacteriologist's last problem; he was free to return to the United States with his means of saving mankind.

Drawing the little metal cylinder from his pocket, he burned the body of the Venerian leader to a heap of ashes, ridding the world of the last invader. Then he turned and entered the glass-lined operating room.

Following the dictates of his Venerian knowledge, he crossed to one of the walls, and drew therefrom a flat, glass vessel, somewhat like a petri dish. This contained bacteria that were harmless in themselves, and were hostile to those of the Gray Plague. These germs, brought from Venus, were the only cure for the terrible disease.[1]

[1] The work of the English bacteriologist Twort, in 1915, and the Frenchman, d'Herelle, in 1917, brought to the attention of the scientific world the fact that many bacteria are subject to attack and destruction by some unknown active agent with which they are associated in infected material. This agent, whatever its character, changed growing germ cultures to a dead, glassy substance.

Twort advanced the thought that the agent might be a living, filtered virus, although he favored the theory that it was an enzyme derived from the bacteria themselves.

D'Herelle, on the contrary, believed that this phenomenon was due to a living, multiplying, ultra-microscopic microbe that destroyed certain bacteria.

Evidence favoring both theories has come to light, with the result that, at present, controversy is rife. Up to date, the contention of neither side has been proved.

Parkinson's adventure was almost at an end. He had not emerged unscathed, but he had won!

The details of his further actions need not be recorded. Suffice it to say that he entered the sphere, carrying his precious, curative germs, arose to the top of the tower, and passed through a round opening in its side. His borrowed knowledge revealed that the car possessed abilities that he had not suspected; with amazing speed he caused it to flash across the Atlantic Ocean to the United States.

There he saw the frightful carnage that the Plague had caused, saw the deserted cities—and was filled with self-reproach because he had not acted sooner.

Across the miles and miles of deserted country he sped, following the fleeing hordes, finally passing over the stragglers and landing in the heart of the congested areas. After making a few inquiries, he returned to the sphere, and continued on toward the West. He landed, finally, outside the city of San Francisco.

A short time later, twisted, deformed, yet triumphant, he was ushered into the presence of the United States government as—the man who had saved the human race.

CHAPTER IV

The terrible days of the Gray Plague ended in mystery. Much that had puzzled the world, Parkinson, with his Venerian knowledge, explained; but there was one thing, the final, enigmatical act in the strange drama, that was as much of a mystery to him as it was to the rest of the world.

Enigma! Of what significance, of what portent—who could tell?

When the great vessel from the United States, equipped to destroy the meteor of the Venetians, neared the great thoque sphere, they came upon a scene quite different from what they had expected. Parkinson, who was on the ship, was more surprised than the rest, for he had definite knowledge of what, in the natural course of events, they should see. For the others there was nothing so very strange in what they saw; Parkinson had lied, that was all.

When the bacteriologist had left the meteor, there had been a high, bronze-colored tower, a burnished lighthouse, covering its entire top. It had been there—but now it was gone! Only the jagged, arched surface of the meteor remained.

They lowered boats and rowed to the strange island. There they saw something that filled them—Parkinson especially—with a very definite uneasiness. The entire top of the meteor was a twisted, fire-blasted mass of bronze-like metal. Where the tower had been, where the shaft had led into the remarkable interplanetary vehicle, there was now a broken expanse of thoque that flashed fire under the rays of the sun.

Something seemed to have melted, to have fused the tower, until it had crumpled, and had run, filling the entrance of the meteor. There was irrefutable evidence to that effect; no one thought otherwise.

But what agency had done this strange thing?

Someone suggested that it might have been the work of some prearranged mechanism. Parkinson shook his head. Had such been the case, his Venerian knowledge would have told him so.

Obviously, nothing of Earth had done it, nothing of Earth—then something of Venus! Inconclusive conjecture, perhaps, but no other explanation offered itself. Something had sealed the contents of the meteor from the sight of man, something with a purpose. From Venus? The thought was logical, to say the least.

Not for long did they remain there beside the Venerian vehicle; there was naught for them to do, so they turned about and headed toward the United States. They bore tidings that were vaguely disturbing, tidings that none were glad to hear. For, according to all indications, something alien to Earth was still within her confines.

Behind it all—the meteors, the Plague, the sealing of the Venerian vehicle—is one fact of great significance. No longer is man alone in the universe; no longer is he in isolation! Out of space came a menace, an intelligence striving to wrest from him his right to rule over Earth. No longer can man in his smug complacency think of himself as being secure in his strength. He has been shown the utter folly of such thinking.

The menace—the invaders from Venus—came, and were destroyed, their purposes defeated. Yet—in the vast reaches of space, in worlds of other dimensions, in the cosmic crucible of life that embodies all creation, there may be other forms of life, other menaces, hovering clouds of death, preparing to sweep down upon Earth to snuff out her life. Who can tell?

And who may say that man is free from the Venerian danger? The strange sealing of the meteor implies that the menace is still present. Who knows but what those inhuman Venerian brutes may even now be planning some new invasion, may be preparing to renew their attack upon Earth?

Time alone will tell.

ROBOT PILOTS FOR AIRCRAFT

Perfection of an automatic mechanical piloting mechanism for airplanes has been achieved after several years of experiment at the royal aircraft establishment of Farnborough.

The apparatus has been successfully tried out on various types of planes—two-seater day bombers, large twin-engine night bombers and big flying boats. Its use as a second or relief pilot on long distance flights by Royal Air Force machines is now being considered.

In every test the robot pilot has steered an accurate course for hours at a time and over distances up to 400 miles while human members of the crew have been concerned with other duties.

The basis of the mechanical pilot is a gyroscope that controls pistons connected with the rudder and elevators of the plane. These pistons are actuated by compressed air.

Once a course is set the robot pilot keeps the machine on that route and errors of even a fraction of a degree are instantly and automatically detected and corrected. All the human pilot has to do in a plane so equipped is to take off and land the machine.

The Pilot's Assister is the official name of the new English device. It weighs about 120 pounds.

Flights have been made with the mechanical pilot in all sorts of weather. In dense fog and clouds, when a human pilot would have found it almost impossible to maintain straight or level flight because of the absence of any visible horizon by which to steer, the mechanical pilot flew the plane with absolute accuracy. On one test flight the automatic pilot steered a dead true course from Farnborough in South England, to Newcastle, 270 miles farther north. The human pilot did not touch the controls until it was necessary to land the plane at the destination.

Hans and I hauled out the heavy casket.

JETTA OF THE LOWLANDS

Conclusion

By Ray Cummings

CHAPTER XV

In the Bandit Camp

The dark cave, with its small spots of tube-light mounted upon movable tripods, was eery with grotesque swaying shadows. The bandit camp. Hidden down here in the depths of the Mid-Atlantic Lowlands. An inaccessible retreat, this cave in what once was the ocean floor. Only a few years ago water had been here, water black and cold and soundless. Tremendous pressure, with three thousand or more fathoms of the ocean above it. Fishes had roamed these passages, no doubt. Strange monsters of the deeps: sightless, or with eyes like phosphorescent torches.

Black-garbed figures move in ghastly greenness as the invisible flyer speeds on its business of ransom.

But the water was gone now. Blue ooze was caked upon the cave floor. Eroded walls; niches and tiny gullies; crevices and an arching dome high overhead. A fantastic cave—no one, seeing it as I saw it that morning at dawn, could have believed it was upon this earth. From where De Boer had put me—on the flat top of a small, butte-like dome near the upper end of the sloping cave floor—all the area of this strange bandit camp was visible to me.

A little tent of parchment was set upon the dome-top.

"Yours," said De Boer, with a grin. "Make yourself comfortable. Gutierrez will be your willing servant, until we see about this ransom. It will have to be one very large, for you are a damn trouble to me, Grant. And a risk. Food will come shortly. Then you can sleep: I think you will want it."

He leaped from the little butte, leaving the taciturn ever-watchful Gutierrez sitting cross-legged on the ledge near me, with his projector across his knees.

The cave was irregularly circular, with perhaps, a hundred-feet diameter and a ceiling fifty feet high. A drift of the fetid, Lowland air went through it—into a rift at this upper end, and out through the lower passage entrance which sloped downward thirty feet and debouched upon a rippled ramp of ooze outside. It was daylight out there now. From my perch I could see the sullen heavy walls of a ridge. Mist hung against them, but the early morning sunlight came down in shafts penetrating the mist and striking the oily surface of a spread of water left here in the depths of a cauldron.

De Boer's flyer was outside. We had landed by the shore of the sea, and the bandits had pushed the vehicle into an arching recess which seemed as though made to hide it. All this camp was hidden. Arching crags of the ridge-wall jutted out over the cave entrance. From above, any passing flyer—even though well below the zero-height—would see nothing but this black breathing sea, lapping against its eroded, fantastic shore-line.

Within the cave, there was only a vague filtering daylight from the lower entrance, a thin shaft from the rift overhead, and the blue tube-light, throwing great shadows of the tents and the men against the black rock walls.

There seemed perhaps a hundred of the bandits here. A semi-permanent camp, by its aspect. Grey parchment tents were set up about the floor, some small, others more elaborate. It seemed as though it were a huddled little group of buildings in the open air, instead of in a cave. One tent, just at the foot of my dome, seemed De Boer's personal room. He went into it after leaving me, and came out to join the main group of his fellows near the center of the cave where a large electron stove, and piped water from a nearby subterranean freshet, and a long table set with glassware and silver, stood these men for kitchen and eating place.

The treasure had not yet been brought in from the flyer. But, from what I overheard, it seemed that the radiumized ingots of the ill-fated Spawn and Perona were to be stored for a year at least, here in this cave. I could see the strong-room cubby. It was hewn from the rock of the cave wall, its sealed-grid door-oval set with metal bars.

I saw also what seemed a small but well-equipped machine shop, in a recess room at one side of the cave. Men were working in there under the light of tubes. And there was a niche hollowed out in the wall to make a room for De Boer's instruments—ether-wave receivers and transmitters, the aerial receiving wires of which stretched in banks along the low ceiling.

There was no activity in there now, except for one man who was operating what I imagined might be an aerial insulator, guarding the place from any prying search-vibrations.

The main cave was a bustle of activity. The arriving bandits were greeting their fellows and exchanging news. The men who had been left here were jubilant at the success of the Chief's latest enterprise. Bottles were unsealed and they began to prepare the morning meal.

My presence caused considerable comment. I was a complication at which most of the men were ill pleased, especially when the arriving bandits told who I was, and that the patrols of the United States were doubtless even now trying to find me.

But De Boer silenced the grumbling with rough words.

"My business, not yours. But you will take your share of his ransom, won't you? Have done!"

And Jetta, she had caused comment also. But when the bottles were well distributed the grumbling turned to ribald banter which made me shudder that it should fall upon Jetta's ears. De Boer had kept his men away from her, shoving them aside when they crowded to see her. She was in a little tent now, not far from the base of my ledge.

My meal presently was brought from where most of the bandits now were roistering at the long table in the center of the cave.

"Eat," said Gutierrez. "I eat with you, Americano. *Madre Mia*, when you are ransomed away from here it will please me! De Boer is fool, with taking such a chance."

With the meal ended, another guard came to take Gutierrez' place and I was ordered into my tent. The routine of the camp, it seemed, was to use the daylight hours for the time of sleep. There were lookouts and guards at the entrance, and a little arsenal of ready weapons stocked in the passage. The men at the table were still at their meal. It would end, I did not doubt, by most of them falling into heavy alcoholic slumber.

I was tired, poisoned by the need of sleep. I lay on fabric cushions piled in one corner of my tent. But sleep would not come; my thoughts ran like a tumbling mountain torrent, and as aimlessly. I hoped that Jetta was sleeping. De Boer was now at the center table with his men. Hans was guarding Jetta. He was a phlegmatic, heavy Dutchman, and seemed decent enough.

I wondered what Hanley might be doing to rescue me. But as I thought about it, I could only hope that his patrols would not find us out here. An attack and most certainly De Boer and his men in their anger would kill me out of hand. And possibly Jetta also.

I had not had a word alone with Jetta since that scene in the control room. When we disembarked, she had stayed close by De Boer. But I knew that Jetta had fathomed my purpose, that she was working to the same end. We must find a way of arranging the ransom which would give us an opportunity to escape.

I pondered it. And at last an idea came to me, vague in all its details, as yet. But it seemed feasible, and I thought it would sound plausible to De Boer. I would watch my chance and explain it to him. Then I realized how much aid Jetta would be. She would agree with my plan, and help me convince him. And when the crucial time came, though I would be a captive, watched by Gutierrez, bound and gagged, perhaps—Jetta would be at liberty. De Boer and Gutierrez would not be on their guard with her.

I drifted off to sleep, working out the details of my plan.

CHAPTER XVI

Planning The Ransom

I was awakened by the sound of low voices outside my tent. Jetta's voice, and De Boer's, and, mingled with them, the babble of the still hilarious bandits in the center of the cave. But there were only a few left now; most of them had fallen into heavy slumber. I had been asleep for several hours, I figured. The daylight shadows outside the cave entrance showed that it was at least noon.

I lay listening to the voices which had awakened me. De Boer was saying:

"But why, Jetta, should I bother with your ideas? I know what is best. This ransom is too dangerous to arrange." His voice sounded calmly good humored; I could hear in it now more than a trace of alcoholic influence. He added, "I think we had better kill him and have done. My men think so, too; already I have caused trouble with them, by bringing him."

It jolted me into full wakefulness.

Jetta's voice: "No! I tell you it can be arranged, Hendrick. I have been thinking of it, planning it—"

"Child! Well what? The least I can do is listen; I am no pig-headed American. Say it out. What would you do to ransom him safely?"

They were just at the foot of my ledge, in front of De Boer's tent. Their voices rose so that I could hear them plainly. For all my start at being awakened to hear my death determined upon, I recall that I was almost equally startled by Jetta's voice. Her tone, her manner with De Boer. Whatever opportunities they had had for talking together, the change in their relationship was remarkable. De Boer was now flushed with drink, but for all that he had obviously still a firm grip upon his wits. And I heard Jetta now urging her ideas upon him with calm confidence. An outward confidence; yet under it there was a vibrant emotion suppressed within her even tone; a hint of tremulous fright; a careful calculation of the effect she might be making upon De Boer. Had he not been intoxicated—with drink and with her—he might have sensed it. But he did not.

"Hendrick, it can be done. A big price. Why not?"

"Because if we are trapped and caught, of what use is the price we might have gotten? Tell me that, wise one?"

"We will not be trapped. And suppose you kill him—won't they track you just the same, Hendrick?"

"No. We would leave his body on some crag where it would be found. The patrols would more quickly tire of chasing a killer when the damage is done. They want Grant alive."

"Then let them have him alive—for a big price. Hendrick, listen—"

"Well, what?" he demanded again. "What is your plan?"

"Why—well, Hendrick, like this—"

She stammered, and I realized that she had no plausible plan. She was fumbling, groping, urging upon De Boer that I must be ransomed alive. But she had not good reason for it.

"Well?" he prompted impatiently.

"You—can you raise Great New York on the audiphone, Hendrick?"

"Yes," he said.

"Hanley's office?"

"Yes, no doubt. Chah—that would give him a start, wouldn't it? De Boer calmly calling him!"

He was laughing. I heard what sounded as though he were gulping another drink. "By damn, Jetta, you are not the timid bird you look. Call Hanley, eh?"

"Yes. Can it be done and still bar his instruments from locating us?"

"Yes, and bar his television. Believe it, Jetta. I have every device for hiding. But—call Hanley!"

"Why not? ... Hendrick, stop!"

I started. It seemed that he was embracing her; forcing half drunken caresses upon her.

I scrambled through my tent doorway, but Gutierrez, who had come back on guard, at once seized me.

"*Hui*—so haste! Back, you."

The Spaniard spoke softly, and he was grinning. "The chief plays with woman's words, no? Charming señorita, though she dresses like a boy. But that is the more charming, eh? Listen to her, Grant."

He gripped me, and prodded my side with the point of his knife blade. "Lie down Americano: we will listen."

Jetta was insisting. "Hendrick, stop!"

"Why?"

I could see them now. They were seated before the opening of De Boer's tent. A little stove in front of them. Coffee for Jetta, who was seated cross-legged, pouring it; a bowl of drink for De Boer. And some baked breadstuff dainties on a platter.

"Hendrick—"

She pushed him away as he leaned to embrace her. Although she was laughing with him, I could only guess at the chill of fear that might be in her heart.

"Foolish, Hendrick!"

"Foolish little bird, Jetta mine."

"You—it is you who are foolish, Hendrick." She slid from his embrace and held her brimming coffee cup balanced before her, to ward him off. "You think I am really clever, so trust me, Hendrick. Oh there is a great future for us: you say I inspire you; let me! Hendrick De Boer, Chieftain of the Lowlands! My father would have helped you become that. You can build a little empire. Hendrick—why not? Father wanted to make you President of Nareda. Why not build your own Lowland Empire? We have a hundred men now? Why not gather a thousand? Ten thousand? An empire!"

"*Ave Maria*," from Gutierrez. "This *niña* thinks big thoughts!"

De Boer raised his bowl. "An empire—De Boer of the Lowlands! Go on; you amuse me. We have a nice start, with this treasure."

"Yes. And the ransom money. But you will take me first to Cape Town, Hendrick? We can be married there: I am seventeen in a month."

"Of course, Jetta. Haven't I promised?" There was no convincingness to me in the way he said it. "Of course. To Cape Town for our marriage."

"Stop! Hendrick, be serious!" He had reached for her again. "Don't be a fool, Hendrick."

"Very well," he said. "I am all serious. What is your plan?"

She was more resourceful this time. She retorted, "This craven Grant, he fears for his life—but he is very smart, Hendrick. I think he is scheming every moment how he can be safely ransomed."

"Hah! No doubt of that!"

"And he has had experience with Chief Hanley. He knows Hanley's methods, how Hanley will act. Let us see what Grant says of this."

She had no plan of her own, but she hoped that by now I had one! And she was making an opportunity for me to put it before De Boer.

He said, "There is sense to that, Jetta. If there is any way to fool Hanley, that craven American has no doubt thought it out."

She held another drink before him. "Yes. Let us see what he says."

He drank; and again as they were near together he caressed her.

"What a schemer you are, little bird. You and I are well matched, eh?"

"Gutierrez may be watching us!" she warned.

They suddenly looked up and saw Gutierrez and me.

"Hah!" Fortunately it struck De Boer into further good humor. "Hah—we have an audience! Bring down the prisoner, Gutierrez! Let us see if his wits can get him out of this plight. Come down, Grant!"

Gutierrez shoved me down the ladder ahead of him. De Boer stood up and seized me. His great fingers dug into my shoulders.

"Sit down, American! It seems you are not to die. *Perhaps* not."

The strength of his fingers was hurting me: he hoped I would wince. Mine was now an ignominious role, indeed, yet I knew it was best.

I gasped. "Don't do that: you hurt!"

He chuckled and cast me loose. I added, with a show of spirit, "You are a bullying giant. Just because you are bigger than I am—"

"Hear that, Jetta? The American finds courage with his coming ransom!"

He shoved me to the ground. Gutierrez grinned, and withdrew a trifle. Jetta avoided meeting my gaze.

"Have some coffee," De Boer offered. "Alcohol is not good for you. Now say: have you any suggestions on how I can safely ransom you?"

It seemed that Jetta was holding her breath with anxiety. But I answered with an appearance of ready eagerness. "Yes. I have. I can arrange it with complete safety to you, if you give me a chance."

"You've got your chance. Speak out."

"You promise you will return me alive? Not hurt me?"

"De duvel—yes! You have my promise. But your plan had better be very good."

"It is."

I told it carefully. The details of it grew with my words. Jetta joined in it. But, most of all, it did indeed sound feasible. "But it must be done at once," I urged. "The weather is right; to-night it will be dark; overcast; not much wind. Don't you think so?"

He sent Gutierrez to the cave's instrument room to read the weather forecast instruments. My guess was right.

"To-night then," I said. "If we linger, it only gives Hanley more time to plan trickery."

"Let us try and raise him now," Jetta suggested.

The Dutchman, Hans, had joined us. He too, seemed to think my ideas were good.

Except for the guards at the cave entrance, all the other bandits were far gone in drink. With Hans and Gutierrez, we went to the instrument room to call Hanley. As we crossed the cave, with Hans and De Boer walking ahead together, De Boer spoke louder than he realized, and the words came back to me.

"Not so bad, Hans? We will use him—but I am not a fool. I'll send him back dead, not alive! A little knife-thrust, just at the end! Safest for us, eh, Hans?"

CHAPTER XVII

Within the Black Sack

We left the bandit stronghold just after nightfall that same day. There were five of us on the X-flyer. Jetta and De Boer, Hans and Gutierrez and myself. The negotiations with Hanley had come through satisfactorily; to De Boer, certainly, for he was in a triumphant mood as they cast off the aero and we rose over the mist-hung depths.

It was part of my plan, this meager manning of the bandit ship. But it was mechanically practical: there was only Hans needed at the controls for this short-time flight: with De Boer plotting his course, working out his last details—and with Gutierrez to guard me.

De Boer had been quite willing to take no other men—and most of them were too far gone in their cups to be of much use. I never have fathomed De Boer's final purpose. He promised Jetta now that when I was successfully ransomed he would proceed to Cape Town by comfortable night flights and marry her. It pleased Gutierrez and Hans, for they wanted none of their comrades. The treasure was still on the flyer. The ransom gold would be added to it. I think that De Boer, Gutierrez and Hans planned never to return to their band. Why, when the treasure divided so nicely among three, break it up to enrich a hundred?

I shall never forget Hanley's grim face as we saw it that afternoon on De Boer's image-grid. My chief sat at his desk with all his location detectors impotent, listening to my disembodied voice explaining what I wanted him to do. My humble, earnest, frightened desire to be ransomed safely at all costs! My plea that he do nothing to try and trap De Boer!

It hurt me to appear so craven. But with it all, I knew that Hanley understood. He could imagine my leering captor standing at my elbow, prompting my words, dictating my very tone—prodding me with a knife in the ribs. I tried, by every shade of meaning, to convey to Hanley that I hoped to escape and save the ransom money. And I think that he guessed it, though he was wary in the tone he used for De Boer to hear. He accepted, unhesitatingly, De Boer's proposition: assured us he would do nothing to assail De Boer; and never once did his grim face convey a hint of anything but complete acquiescence.

We had President Markes on the circuit. De Boer, with nothing to lose, promised to return Jetta with me. In gold coin, sixty thousand U. S. dollar-standards for me; a third as much from Nareda, for Jetta.

The details were swiftly arranged. We cut the circuit. I had a last look at Hanley's face as the image of it faded. He seemed trying to tell me to do the best I could; that he was powerless, and would do nothing to jeopardize my life and Jetta's. Everything was ready for the affair to be consummated at once. The weather was right; there was time for Hanley and De Boer each comfortably to reach the assigned meeting place.

We flew, for the first hour, nearly due west. The meeting place was at 35 deg. N. by 59 deg. W., a few hundred miles east by north of the fairy-like mountaintop of the Bermudas. Our charts showed the Lowlands there to run down to what once was measured as nearly three thousand fathoms—called now eighteen thousand feet below the zero-height. A broken region, a depth-ridge fairly level, and no Lowland sea, nor any settlements in the neighborhood.

The time was set at an hour before midnight. No mail, passenger or freight flyers were scheduled to pass near there at that hour, and, save for some chance private craft, we would be undisturbed. The ransom gold was available to Hanley. He had said he would bring it in his personal Wasp.

The details of the exchange were simple. Hanley, with only one mechanic, would hover at the zero-height, his Wasp lighted so that we could see it plainly. The wind drift, according to forecast, would be southerly. At 11 P.M. Hanley would release from his Wasp a small helium-gas baloon-car—a ten-foot basket with the supporting gas bag above it, weighted so that it would slowly descend into the depths, with a southern drift.

Our flyer, invisible and soundless, would pick up the baloon-car at some point in its descent. The gold would be there, in a black casket. De Boer would take the gold, deposit Jetta and me in the car, and release it again. And when the balloon finally settled to the rocks beneath, Hanley could pick it up. No men would be hidden by Hanley in that basket. De Boer had stipulated that when casting loose the balloon, its car must be swept by Hanley with a visible electronic ray. No hidden men could withstand that blast!

Such was the arrangement with Hanley. I was convinced that he intended to carry it out to the letter. He would have his own invisible X-flyer in the neighborhood, no doubt. But it would not interfere with the safe transfer of Jetta and me.

That De Boer would carry out his part, Hanley could only trust. He had said so this afternoon bluntly. And De Boer had laughed and interposed his voice in our circuit.

"Government money against these two lives, Hanley! Of course you have to trust me!"

It was a flight, for us, of something less than four hours to the meeting place. Hans was piloting, seated alone in the little cubby upon the forward wing-base, directly over the control room. De Boer, with Jetta at his side, worked over his course and watched his instrument banks. I was, at the start of the flight, lashed in a chair of the control room, my ankles and wrists tied and Gutierrez guarding me.

Jetta did not seem to notice me. She did not look at me, nor I at her. She pretended interest only in the success of the transfer; in her father's treasure on board, the coming ransom money, and then a flight to Cape Town, dividing the treasure only with Hans and Gutierrez; and in her marriage with De Boer. She said she wanted me returned to Hanley alive; craven coward that I was, still I did not deserve death. De Boer had agreed. But I knew that at last, as they tumbled me into the basket, someone would slip a knife into me!

I had, as we came on board, just the chance for a few whispered sentences with Jetta. But they were enough! We both knew what we had to do. Desperate expedient, indeed! It seemed more desperate now as the time approached than it had when I planned it.

The weather at 7 P.M. was heavily overcast. Sultry, breathless, with solid, wide-flung cloud areas spread low over the zero-height. Night settled black in the Lowlands. The mists gathered.

We flew well down—under the minus two thousand-foot level—so that out of the mists the highest dome peaks often passed close beneath us.

At 8 P.M. De Boer flung on the mechanism of invisibility. The interior of the ship faded to its gruesome green darkness. My senses reeled as the current surged through me. Lashed in my chair, I sat straining my adjusting eyes, straining my hearing to cope with this gruesome unreality. And my heart was pounding. Would Jetta and I succeed? Or was our love—unspoken love, born of a glance and the pressure of our hands in that moonlit Nareda garden—was our love star-crossed, foredoomed to tragedy? A few hours, now, would tell us.

De Boer was taking no chances. He was using his greatest intensity of power, with every safeguard for complete invisibility and silence. From where I sat I could make out the black form of Hans through the ceiling grid, at his pilot controls in the overhead cubby. A queer glow like an aura was around him. The same green radiance suffused the control room. It could not penetrate the opened windows of the ship; could not pass beyond the electro-magnetic field enveloping us. Nor could the curious hum which permeated the ship's interior get past the barrage barrier. From outside, I knew, we were invisible and inaudible.

Strange unreality, here in the control room! The black-garbed figures of De Boer and Jetta at their table were unreal, spectral. At the door oval, which I could barely see, Gutierrez lurked like a shadow. All of them, and Hans in the cubby above, were garbed in tight-fitting dead-black suits of silklene fabric. Thin, elastic as sheer silk web, opaque, lustreless. It covered their feet, legs and bodies; and their arms and hands like black, silk gloves. Their heads were helmeted with it. And they had black masks which as yet were flapped up and fastened to the helmet above their foreheads. Their faces only were exposed, tinted a ghastly, lurid green by this strange light. It glowed and glistened like phosphorescence on their eyeballs, making them the eyes of animals in a hunter's torchlight, at night.

De Boer moved upon an errand across the control room. He was a burly black spectre in the skin-tight suit. His footfalls faintly sounded on the metal floor. They were toneless footfalls. Unreal. They might have been bells, or jangling thuds; they had lost their identity in this soundless, vibrating hum.

And he spoke, "We are making good progress, Jetta. We will be on time."

Ghastly voice! So devoid of every human timbre, every overtone shade to give it meaning, that it might have been a man's voice, or a woman's, the voice of something living, or something dead. Sepulchral. A stripped shell of voice. Yet to me, inside here with it, it was perfectly audible.

And Jetta said, "Yes, Hendrick, that is good."

A voice like his: no different.

Gruesome. Weird.

I try now to picture the scene in detail, for out of these strange conditions Jetta and I were to make our opportunity.

9 P.M. De Boer was a methodical fellow. He checked his position on the chart. He signalled the routine orders to Hans. And he gestured to Gutierrez. The movements and acts of everyone had been definitely planned. And this, too, Jetta and I had anticipated.

"Time to make him ready, Gutierrez. Bring the sack in here. I'll fasten him away."

I was not garbed like the others. They could move out on the wing runway under Hanley's eyes at short range, or climb in and out of the balloon car, and not be visible.

Gutierrez brought the sack. A dead-black fabric.

"Shall I cut him loose now from his chair, Commander?"

"I'll do it."

De Boer drew a long knife blade, coated black, and thin and sharp as a half-length rapier. Gutierrez had one of similar fashion. No electronic weapons were in evidence, probably because the hiss of one fired would have been too loud for our barrage, and its flash too bright. But a knife thrust is dark and silent!

The Spaniard's eyes were gleaming as he approached me with the bag, as though he were thinking of that silent knife thrust he would give me at the last.

Dr. Boer said, "Stand up, Grant." He cut the fastenings that held me in my chair. But my ankles and wrists remained tied.

"Stand up, can't you?"

"Yes."

I got unsteadily to my feet. In the blurred green darkness I could see that Jetta was not looking at me. Gutierrez held the mouth of the sack open. As though I were an upright log of wood, De Boer lifted me.

"Pull it up over his feet, Gutierrez."

The oblong sack was longer than my body. They drew it over me, and bunched its top over my head. And De Boer laid me none too gently on the floor.

"Lie still. Do you get enough air?"

"Yes."

The black fabric was sufficiently porous for me to breathe comfortably inside the sack.

"All right, Gutierrez, I have the gag."

I felt them carrying me from the control room, twenty feet or so along the corridor, where a door-porte opened to a small balcony runway hung beneath the forward wing. Jutting from it was a little take-off platform some six feet by twelve in size. It was here that the balloon-basket was to be boarded. The casket containing the ransom gold would be landed here, and the sack containing me placed in the car and cast loose. It was all within the area of invisibility of our flyer.

De Boer knelt over me, and drew back the top of the sack to expose my face.

"A little gag for you, Grant, so you will not be tempted to call out."

"I won't do that."

"You might. Well, good-by, American."

"Good-by." And I breathed, "Good-by Jetta." Would I ever see her again? Was this the end of everything for us?

He forced the gag into my mouth, tied it, and verified that my ankles and wrists were securely lashed. In the green radiance he and Gutierrez were like ghouls prowling over me, and their muffled toneless voices, tomblike.

The sack came up over my head.

"Good-by, Grant." I could not tell which one said it. And the other chuckled.

I could feel them tying the mouth of the sack above my head. I lay stiff. Then I heard their steps. Then silence.

I moved. I might have rolled, but I did not try it. I could raise my knees within the sack—double up like a folded pocket knife—but that was all.

A long, dark silence. It seemed interminable. Was Gutierrez guarding me here in the corridor? I could not tell; I heard nothing save the vague hum of the electronite current.

It had been 9 o'clock. Then I fancied that it must be 10. And then, perhaps, almost 11. I wondered what the weather outside was like. Soon we would be nearing the meeting place. Would Hanley be there? Would Jetta soon, very soon now, be able to do her part? I listened, horribly tense, with every interval between the thumps of my heart seeming so long a gap of waiting.

I heard a sound! A toneless, unidentifiable sound. Another like it; a little sequence of faint sounds. Growing louder. Approaching footsteps? Jetta's? I prayed so.

Then a low voice. Two voices. Both the same in quality. But from the words I could identify them.

"Hello, Gutierrez."

"*Niña*, hello."

Jetta! She had come!

"The captive is safe? No trouble?"

"No. He has not moved."

"Careful of him, Gutierrez. He is worth a lot of money to us."

"Well you say it. Señorita. In half an hour now, we will be away. Santa Maria, when this is over I shall breathe with more comfort!"

"We'll have no trouble, Gutierrez. We're almost there. In ten minutes now, or a little more."

"So soon? What time is it?"

"Well, after half-past ten. When it's over, Gutierrez, we head for Cape Town. Clever of me, don't you think, to persuade Hendrick to take us to Cape Town? Just you three men to divide all this treasure. It would be foolish to let a hundred others have it."

"True, *Niña*; true enough."

"I insisted upon you and Hans—Gutierrez, what is that?"

A silence.

"I heard nothing."

"A voice, was it?"

"The Americano?"

"No! No—the commander calling? Was it? Calling you, Gutierrez? Perhaps we have sighted Hanley's Wasp. Go! I'll stand here, and come quickly back."

Footsteps. Now! Our chance, come at last! I twisted over on my side, and lay motionless. Ah, if only those were Gutierrez' fading footfalls! And Jetta, here alone with me in the green darkness! Just for this one vital moment.

Fingers were fumbling at the top of my sack, unfastening the cord. Hands and arms came swiftly in. Fingers ran down my back as I lay on my side to admit them quickly. Fingers went fumbling at the cords that lashed my crossed wrists behind me. A knee pressed against me. A hurried, panting, half sobbing breath close over me—

Just a hurried moment. The hands withdrew. The sack went back over my head. The knees, the slight weight against me, was gone. A few seconds only.

Footsteps. The voices again.

"Was it the commander, Gutierrez?"

"No. I do not know what it was. Nothing, probably."

"The Wasp in sight?"

"Not yet, *Niña*. You had best go back: De Boer, he might be jealous of us, no? He is busy with his instruments, but should he realize you are here, talking with me—"

"Senseless, Gutierrez!"

"Is it so, *Niña*? I have no attraction? Go back to him. Gold I want, not trouble over you!"

Faint laughter.

"When we sight the Wasp, I'll call and tell you, Gutierrez. Too bad you won't let me stay with you. I like you."

"Yes. But go now!"

Faint laughter. Footsteps. Then silence.

Our vital moment had come and passed. And Jetta had done her part; the role of action upon this dim lurid stage was now mine to play.

My hands were free.

CHAPTER XVIII

The Combat in the Green Darkness

Another interval. A dead, dark silence. I did not dare move. Gutierrez was here, within a few feet of me, probably. I wondered if he could see the outlines of the black sack. Doubtless they were very vague. But if I exposed my flesh, my face, my hands, that would at once attract his attention.

I worked the loosened cords from my wrists; moved my stiffened hands until, with returning blood, the strength came to them. I could not reach my bound ankles without doubling up my knees. I did not dare chance such a movement of the sack. But, after a moment, I got my hands in front of me.

Then I took the gag from my mouth and, with a cautious hand, pried at the top of the sack where it was bunched over my head. Its fastening was loose.

Another interval. A dim muffled voice; "The Wasp is in sight, Gutierrez!"

A movement—a sound like footsteps. Probably Gutierrez moving to the corridor window to glance at Hanley's distant hovering flyer. I hoped it might be that: I had to take the chance.

I slid the bag from my face. I feared an abrupt alarm, or Gutierrez leaping upon me. But there was silence, and I saw his vague dark outlines at the window oval, five feet from me.

I got my ankles loose and slid the bag off. I was unsteady on my feet, but desperation aided me.

Gutierrez half turned as I gripped him from behind. My hand on his mouth stifled his outcry. His black knife blade waved blindly. Then my clenched knuckle caught his temple, and dug with the twisting Santus blow. I was expert at it, and I found the vulnerable spot.

He crumpled in my grasp, and I slid his falling body across the narrow corridor into the nearest cubby oval.

Almost soundless; and in the control room Jetta and De Boer were murmuring and gazing at Hanley's ship, which hung ahead and above us at the zero-height.

I had planned all my movements. No motion was lost. Gutierrez was about my height and build. I stripped his black suit from him, donned it, then tied his ankles and wrists, and gagged him against the time when he would recover consciousness. Then I stuffed his body in the sack and tied its top.

This black suit had a mask, rolled up and fastened to the helmet. I loosed it, dropping it over my face. Knife in hand, I stood at the corridor window.

It was all black outside. The clouds were black overhead; the highest Lowland crags, several thousand feet beneath us, were all but blotted out in the murky darkness. Only one thing was to be seen: a quarter of a mile ahead, now, and a thousand feet higher than our level, the shining, bird-like outlines of Hanley's hovering little Wasp. It stood like a painted image of an aero, alone on a dead-black background. Red and green signal-lights dotted it, and on its stern tip a small, spreading searchlight bathed the wings and the body with a revealing silver radiance.

Our forward flight had been checked, and we, too, were hovering. Hans doubtless would remain for a time in the pilot cubby; De Boer and Jetta were in the control room. It was only twenty feet away, but I could barely see its oval entrance.

"Gutierrez!"

One of them was calling. My hollow empty voice echoed back as I softly responded:

"Yes?"

"Be ready. We are arrived."

"Yes, Commander. All is well."

I continued to stand at the window. Hanley's little balloon-car was visible now. Then he cut it away. We had moved forward in the interval. The tiny car floated out almost above us.

My gaze searched the void of darkness outside. Did Hanley have an invisible flyer out there? Perhaps so. But it could accomplish nothing as yet. It would not even dare approach, for fear of collision with us.

The tiny car, with a white pilot light in it, swayed with a slow descent. The basket beneath the supporting balloon oscillated in a wide swing, then steadied. A sudden flash showed up there—a flashing electronic stream, from Hanley's Wasp to the basket. The shot swept the basket interior. No one could be hidden there and survive.

It was Hanley's proof to us that he was following instructions.

"Hah! He obeys properly, Jetta!"

The voice floated back to me from the control room. Could I creep in there, surprise De Boer now, and kill him? Doubtless. But it would alarm Hans. I must await my chance to get them together.

"Gutierrez! Hans, get us under it! Gutierrez!"

The vague outline of De Boer came toward me in the corridor, burly dark blob. His mask was down now. There were points of light, glowing like faint distant stars, to mark his eyes.

"Gutierrez."

"Yes."

A small black figure followed after him. Jetta.

"Yes, De Boer." I stood over the sack. "I am ready."

De Boer's giant shape towered beside me. Now! My knife thrust now! But Hans was coming toward us. He would take alarm before I could reach him.

"Open the side porte, Gutierrez. Hurry, the car is here. Hans, you should have stayed up there!"

"The drift is calculated; the car is just here."

We were all swift-moving shadows; disembodied voices.

"Get that porte open."

"Yes." I opened it.

We went outside on the runway. I passed close to Jetta, and just for an instant pressed my gloved fingers on the black fabric of her arm—and she knew.

"Now, seize it."

"Here, Hans, climb up."

"I have it. Pull it, Gutierrez!"

The car drifted at us from the black void. We caught it.

"Hold it, Gutierrez."

"Hans, clip the balloon. Up with you."

In the blurred haste, I could not get them together. I did not want to kill one and have the other leap upon me.

We fastened the little balloon and dragged the car onto the take-off platform. The shape of Hans leaped into the car.

"It is here! The ransom money!"

"Lift it to me. Heavy?"

"Yes."

"Gutierrez, help me. Hurry! If Hanley tries any trickery—"

Our aero was drifting downward and southward in the slight wind. Hanley's Wasp still hovered at the zero-height.

"In, Gutierrez."

Hans and I hauled out the heavy casket and placed it on the wing runway. De Boer pried up its lid. The gold was there. I could not tell where Jetta was; I prayed she would keep away from this.

Then the shape of De Boer was missing! But in a moment he appeared, dragging the sack.

"Lift him, Gutierrez. Hans, unclip the balloon and shove off the car!"

We were all standing at the two-foot rail of the runway. The car-basket, floating now, was off side and level with us. My chance!

"In with him, Gutierrez."

I shoved the body, encased in its black sack, with Hans helping me. And suddenly De Boer's knife came down at the sack! A stab. But an instinct to save the poor wretch within swept me. I struck at De Boer's arm and deflected the blow. The sack tumbled into the car.

I had neglected whatever chance had existed. Too late now!

"What in the hell!"

De Boer's shape seized me.

"What—"

It sent me into a sudden confusion. I flung him off. I stumbled against the shape of Hans.

The car was almost loose; drifting away.

Without thought—a frantic impulse—I pushed Hans over the brink. He fell into the car. It swayed into an oscillation with the impact. The balloon sank below our wing level and was gone, with only Hans, muffled shouts floating up.

And De Boer came leaping at me from behind. I whirled around. My danger was too much for the watching Jetta. She screamed.

"Philip, look out for him!"

"Hah! The American. By damn, what is this?"

It gave De Boer pause. He gripped a wing stay-wire for a second.

Then he came with a rush.

The corridor door was open behind me. I flung myself into it—and collided with a shape.

"Philip!"

I shoved at her frantically.

"Jetta, get back! Away from us!"

I pulled at her, half falling. De Boer's shape came through the doorway into the corridor. And was blotted out in the green darkness as he turned the other way, to avoid me if I struck.

A silence. The shadow of Jetta was behind me. I stood with poised knife, listening, straining my eyes through the faint green darkness. De Boer was here, knife in hand, fallen now into craftly, motionless silence. He might have been close here down the corridor. Or in any one of these nearby cubby doorways.

I slid forward along the wall. The corridor was solid black down its length: the green radiance seemed brighter at the control room behind me. Had De Boer gone into this solid blackness, to lure me?

I stopped my advance. Stood again, trying to see or hear something.

And then I saw him! Two small glowing points of light. Distant stars. His eyes! Five feet ahead of me? Or ten? Or twenty?

A rustle. A sound.

His dark form materialized as he came—a huge, black blob overwhelming me, his arm and knife blade striking.

I dropped to the floor-grid, and his blade went over me. And as I dropped, I struck with an upward thrust. My knife met solidity; sank into flesh.

I twisted past him on the floor as he fell. My knife was gone: buried in him.

Words were audible; choking gasps. I could see his form rising, staggering. The open porte was near him; he swayed through it.

Did he know he was mortally wounded? I think so. He swayed on the wing runway, and I slid to the door and stood watching. And was aware of the shadow of Jetta creeping to join me.

"Is he—?"

"Quiet, Jetta."

He stood under the wing, swaying, gripping a stay. Then his voice sounded, and it seemed like a laugh.

"The craven American—wins." He moved a step. "Not to see—me die—"

He toppled at the rail. "Good-by, Jetta."

A great huddled shadow. A blob, toppling, falling....

Far down there now the crags and peaks of the Lowland depths were visible. The darkness swallowed his whirling body. We could not hear the impact.

CHAPTER XIX

Episode of the Lowlands

There is but little remaining for me to record. I could not operate the mechanism of invisibility of De Boer's X-flyer. But its pilot controls were simple. With Jetta at my side, trembling now that our gruesome task was over, we groped our way through the green darkness and mounted to the pilot cubby. And within ten minutes I had lowered the ship into the depths, found a landing place upon the dark rocks, and brought us down.

Hanley's Wasp had landed: we saw its lights half a mile from us. And then the lights of another ship—an X-flyer convoying Hanley—slowly materializing nearby.

And then reunion. Jetta and I left De Boer's invisible vessel and clambered over the rocks. And presently Hanley, staring at our grotesque black forms, came rushing forward and greeted us.

We were an hour locating De Boer's flyer, for all that Jetta and I had just left it and thought we could find our way back. But we stumbled onto it at last. Hanley felt his way aboard and brought it to visibility. It has since been returned to the Anti-War Department, with the compliments of Hanley's Office.

The ransom money was restored to its proper source. Spawn's treasure of radiumized quicksilver we shipped back to Nareda, where it was checked and divided, and Jetta's share legally awarded to her.

De Boer was dead when Hanley found him that night on the rocks. Jetta and I did not go to look at him....

The balloon basket landed safely. Hanley and his men were down there in time to seize it. Hans was caught; and Gutierrez, within the sack, was found to be uninjured. They are incarcerated now in Nareda. They were willing to tell the location of the bandit stronghold. A raid there the following day resulted in the capture of most of De Boer's men.

All this is now public news. You have heard it, of course. Yet in my narrative, setting down the events as I lived them, I have tried to give more vivid details than the bare facts as they were blared through the public audiphones.

An episode of the strange, romantic, fantastic Lowlands. A very unimportant series of incidents mingled with the news of a busy world—just a few minutes of the newscasters' time to tell how a band of depth smugglers was caught.

But it was a very important episode to me. It changed, for me, a clanking, thrumming machine-made world into a shining fairyland of dreams come true. It gave me little Jetta.

(THE END)

Carr went mad with fury. There it was, looming close in his vision.

VAGABONDS OF SPACE

A COMPLETE NOVELETTE

By Harl Vincent

CHAPTER I

The Nomad

Gathered around a long table in a luxuriously furnished director's room, a group of men listened in astonishment to the rapid and forceful speech of one of their number.

From the depths of the Sargasso Sea of Space came the thought-warning, "Turn back!" But Carr and his Martian friend found it was too late!

"I tell you I'm through, gentlemen," averred the speaker. "I'm fed up with the job, that's all. Since 2317 you've had me sitting at the helm of International Airways and I've worked my fool head off for you. Now—get someone else!"

"Made plenty of money yourself, didn't you, Carr?" asked one of the directors, a corpulent man with a self-satisfied countenance.

"Sure I did. That's not the point. I've done all the work. There's not another executive in the outfit whose job is more than a title, and you know it. I want a change and a rest. Going to take it, too. So, go ahead with your election of officers and leave me out."

"Your stock?" Courtney Davis, chairman of the board, sensed that Carr Parker meant what he said.

"I'll hold it. The rest of you can vote it as you choose: divide the proxies pro rata, based on your individual holdings. But I reserve the right to dump it all on the market at the first sign of shady dealings. That suit you?"

The recalcitrant young President of International Airways had risen from the table. The chairman attempted to restrain him.

"Come on now, Carr, let's reason this out. Perhaps if you just took a leave of absence—"

"Call it anything you want. I'm done right now."

Carr Parker stalked from the room, leaving eleven perspiring capitalists to argue over his action.

He rushed to the corridor and nervously pressed the call button of the elevators. A minute later he emerged upon the roof of the Airways building, one of the tallest of New York's mid-town sky-scrapers. The air here, fifteen hundred feet above the hot street, was cool and fresh. He walked across the great flat surface of the landing stage to inspect a tiny helicopter which had just settled to a landing. Angered as he was, he still could not resist the attraction these trim little craft had always held for him. The feeling was in his blood.

His interest, however, was short lived and he strolled to the observation aisle along the edge of the landing stage. He stared moodily into the heavens where thousands of aircraft of all descriptions sped hither and yon. A huge liner of the Martian route was dropping from the skies and drifting toward her cradle on Long Island. He looked out over the city to the north: fifty miles of it he knew stretched along the east shore of the Hudson. Greatest of the cities of the world, it housed a fifth of the population of the United States of North America; a third of the wealth.

Cities! The entire world lived in them! Civilization was too highly developed nowadays. Adventure was a thing of the past. Of course there were the other planets, Mars and Venus, but they were as bad. At least he had found them so on his every business trip. He wished he had lived a couple of centuries ago, when the first space-ships ventured forth from the earth. Those were days of excitement and daring enterprise. Then a man could find ways of getting away from things—next to nature—out into the forests; hunting; fishing. But the forests were gone, the streams enslaved by the power monopolies. There were only the cities—and barren plains. Everything in life was made by man, artificial.

Something drew his eyes upward and he spotted an unusual object in the heavens, a mere speck as yet but drawing swiftly in from the upper air lanes. But this ship, small though it appeared, stood out from amongst its fellows for some reason. Carr rubbed his eyes to clear his vision. Was it? Yes—it was—surrounded by a luminous haze. Notwithstanding the brilliance of the afternoon sun, this haze was clearly visible. A silver shimmering that was not like anything he had seen on Earth. The ship swung in toward the city and was losing altitude rapidly. Its silvery aura deserted it and the vessel was revealed as a sleek, tapered cylinder with no wings, rudders or helicopter screws. Like the giant liners of the Interplanetary Service it displayed no visible means of support or propulsion. This was no ordinary vessel.

Carr watched in extreme interest as it circled the city in a huge spiral, settling lower at each turn. It seemed that the pilot was searching for a definite landing stage. Then suddenly it swooped with a rush. Straight for the stage of the Airways building! The strange aura reappeared and the little vessel halted in mid-air, poised a moment, then dropped gracefully and lightly as a feather to the level surface not a hundred feet from where he stood. He hurried to the spot to examine the strange craft.

"Mado!" he exclaimed in surprise as a husky, bronzed Martian squeezed through the quickly opened manhole and clambered heavily to the platform. Mado of Canax—an old friend!

"Devils of Terra!" gasped the Martian, his knees giving way, "—your murderous gravity! Here, help me. I've forgotten the energizing switch."

Carr laughed as he fumbled with a mechanism that was strapped to the Martian's back. Mado, who tipped the scales at over two hundred pounds on his own planet, weighed nearly six hundred here. His legs simply couldn't carry the load!

"There you are, old man." Parker had located the switch and a musical purr came from the black box between the Martian's broad shoulders. "Now stand up and tell me what you're doing here. And what's the idea of the private ship? Come all the way from home in it?"

His friend struggled to his feet with an effort, for the field emanating from the black box required a few seconds to reach the intensity necessary to counteract two-thirds of the earth's gravity.

"Thanks Carr," he grinned. "Yes, I came all the way in that bus. Alone, too—and she's mine! What do you think of her?"

"A peach, from what I can see. But how come? Not using a private space-flier on your business trips, are you?"

"Not on your life! I've retired. Going to play around for a few years. That's why I bought the Nomad."

"Retired! Why Mado, I just did the same thing."

"Great stuff! They've worked you to death. What are you figuring on doing with yourself?"

Carr shrugged his shoulders resignedly. "Usual thing, I suppose. Travel aimlessly, and bore myself into old age. Nothing else to do. No kick out of life these days at all, Mado, even in chasing around from planet to planet. They're all the same."

The Martian looked keenly at his friend. "Oh, is that so?" he said. "No kick, eh? Well, let me tell you, Carr Parker, you come with me and we'll find something you'll get a kick out of. Ever seen the Sargasso Sea of the solar system? Ever been on one of the asteroids? Ever seen the other side of the Moon—Uranus—Neptune—Planet 9, the farthest out from the sun?"

"No-o." Carr's eyes brightened somewhat.

"Then you haven't seen anything or been anywhere. Trouble with you is you've been in the rut too long. Thinking there's nothing left in the universe but the commonplace. Right, too, if you stick to the regular routes of travel. But the *Nomad's* different. I'm just a rover when I'm at her controls, a vagabond in space—free as the ether that surrounds her air-tight hull. And, take it from me, there's something to see and do out there in space. Off the usual lanes, perhaps, but it's there."

"You've been out—how long?" Carr hesitated.

"Eighty Martian days. Seen plenty too." He waved his arm in a gesture that seemed to take in the entire universe.

"Why come here, with so much to be seen out there?"

"Came to visit you, old stick-in-the-mud," grinned Mado, "and to try and persuade you to join me. I find you footloose already. You're itching for adventure; excitement. Will you come?"

Carr listened spellbound. "Right now?" he asked.

"This very minute. Come on."

"My bag," objected Carr, "it must be packed. I'll need funds too."

"Bag! What for? Plenty of duds on the *Nomad*—for any old climate. And money—don't make me laugh! Vagabonds need money?" He backed toward the open manhole of the *Nomad*, still grinning.

Carr hesitated, resisting the impulse to take Mado at his word. He looked around. The landing stage had been deserted, but people now were approaching. People not to be tolerated at the moment. He saw Courtney Davis, grim and determined. There'd be more arguments, useless but aggravating. Well, why not go? He'd decided to break away. What better chance? Suddenly he dived for the manhole of Mado's vessel; wriggled his way to the padded interior of the air-lock. He heard the clang of the circular cover. Mado was clamping it to its gasketed seat.

"Let's go!" he shouted.

CHAPTER II

Into the Heavens

The directors of International Airways stared foolishly when they saw Carr Parker and the giant Martian enter the mysterious ship which was a trespasser on their landing stage. They gazed incredulously as the gleaming torpedo-shaped vessel arose majestically from its position. There was no evidence of motive power other than a sudden radiation from its hull plates of faintly crackling streamers of silvery light. They fell back in alarm as it pointed its nose skyward and accelerated with incredible rapidity, the silver energy bathing them in its blinding luminescence. They burst forth in excited recrimination when it vanished into the blue. Courtney Davis shook his fist after the departing vessel and swore mightily.

Carr Parker forgot them entirely when he clambered into the bucket seat beside Mado, who sat at the Nomad's controls. He was free at last: free to probe the mysteries of outer space, to roam the skies with this Martian he had admired since boyhood.

"Glad you came?" Mado asked his Terrestrial friend.

"You bet. But tell me about yourself. How you've been and how come you've rebelled, too? I haven't seen you for a long time, you know. Why, it's been years!"

"Oh, I'm all right. Guess I got fed up with things about the same way you did. Knew last time I saw you that you were feeling as I did. That's why I came after you."

"But this vessel, the *Nomad*. I didn't know such a thing was in existence. How does it operate? It seems quite different from the usual ether-liners."

“It's a mystery ship. Invented and built by Thrygis, a discredited scientist of my country. Spent a fortune on it and then went broke and killed himself. I bought it from the executors for a song. They thought it was a pile of junk. But the plans and notes of the inventor were there and I studied 'em well. The ship is a marvel, Carr. Utilizes gravitational attraction and reversal as a propelling force and can go like the Old Boy himself. I've hit two thousand miles a second with her."

"A second! Why, that's ten times as fast as the regular liners! Must use a whale of a lot of fuel. And where do you keep it? The fuel, I mean."

"Make it right on board. I'm telling you Carr, the *Nomad* has no equal. She's a corker."

"I'll say she is. But what do you mean—make the fuel?"

"Cosmic rays. Everywhere in space you know. Seems they are the result of violent concentrations of energy that cause the birth of atoms. Thrygis doped out a collector of these rays that takes 'em from their paths and concentrates 'em in a retort where there's a spongy metal catalyst that never deteriorates. Here there is a reaction to the original action out in space and new atoms are born, simple ones of hydrogen. But what could be sweeter for use in one of our regular atomic motors? The energy of disintegration is used to drive the generators of the artificial gravity field, and there you are. Sounds complicated, but really isn't. And nothing to get out of whack either."

"Beats the rocket motors and bulky fuel of the regular liners a mile, doesn't it? But since when are you a navigator, Mado?"

"Don't need to be a navigator with the *Nomad.* She's automatic, once the controls are set. Say we wish to visit Venus. The telescope is sighted on that body and the gravity forces adjusted so we'll be attracted in that direction and repelled in the opposite direction. Then we can go to bed and forget it. The movement of the body in its orbit makes no difference because the force follows wherever it goes. See? The speed increases until the opposing forces are equal, when deceleration commences and we gradually slow down until within ten thousand miles of the body, when the *Nomad* automatically stops. Doesn't move either, until we awaken to take the controls. How's that for simple?"

"Good enough. But suppose a wandering meteor or a tiny asteroid gets in the way? At our speed it wouldn't have to be as big as your fist to go through us like a shot."

"All taken care of, my dear Carr. I told you Thrygis was a wiz. Such a happenstance would disturb the delicate balance of the energy compensators and the course of the *Nomad* would instantly alter to dodge the foreign object. Once passed by, the course would again be resumed."

"Some ship, the *Nomad*!" Carr was delighted with the explanations. "I'm sold on her and on the trip. Where are we now and where bound?"

Mado glanced at the instrument board. "Nearly a million miles out and headed for that Sargasso Sea I told you about," he said. "It isn't visible in the telescope, but I've got it marked by the stars. Out between the orbits of Mars and Jupiter, a quarter of a billion miles away. But we'll average better than a thousand miles a second. Be there in three days of your time."

"How can there be a sea out there in space?"

"Oh, that's just my name for it. Most peculiar thing, though. There's a vast, billowy sort of a cloud. Twists and weaves around as if alive. Looks like seaweed or something; and Carr, I swear there are things floating around in it. Wrecks. Something damn peculiar, anyway. I vow I saw a signal. People marooned there or something. Sorta scared me and I didn't stay around for long as there was an awful pull from the mass. Had to use full reversal of the gravity force to get away."

"Now why didn't you tell me that before? That's something to think about. Like the ancient days of ocean-going ships on Earth."

"Tell you? How could I tell you? You've been questioning me ever since I first saw you and I've been busy every minute answering you."

Carr laughed and slid from his seat to the floor. He felt curiously light and loose-jointed. A single step carried him to one of the stanchions of the control cabin and he clung to it for a moment to regain his equilibrium.

"What's wrong?" he demanded. "No internal gravity mechanism on the *Nomad*?"

"Sure is. But it's adjusted for Martian gravity. You'll get along, but it wouldn't be so easy for me with Earth gravity. I'd have to wear the portable G-ray all the time, and that's not so comfortable. All right with you?"

"Oh, certainly. I didn't understand."

Carr saw that his friend had unstrapped the black box from his shoulders. He didn't blame him. Glad he wasn't a Martian. It was mighty inconvenient for them on Venus or Terra. Their bodies, large and of double the specific gravity, were not easily handled where gravity was nearly three times their own. The Venusians and Terrestrials were more fortunate when on Mars, for they could become accustomed to the altered conditions. Only had to be careful they didn't overdo. He remembered vividly a quick move he had made on his first visit to Mars. Carried him twenty feet to slam against a granite pedestal. Bad cut that gave him, and the exertion in the rarefied atmosphere had him gasping painfully.

He walked to one of the ports and peered through its thick window. Mado was fussing with the controls. The velvety blackness of the heavens; the myriad diamond points of clear brilliance. Cold, too, it looked out there, and awesomely vast. The sun and Earth had been left behind and could not be seen. But Carr didn't care. The heavens were marvelous when viewed without the obstruction of an atmosphere. But he'd seen them often enough on his many business trips to Mars and Venus.

"Ready for bed?" Mado startled him with a tap on the shoulder.

"Why—if you say so. But you haven't shown me through the *Nomad* yet."

"All the time in the universe for that. Man, don't you realize you're free? Come, let's grab some sleep. Need it out here. The ship'll be here when we wake up. She's flying herself right now. Fast, too."

Carr looked at the velocity indicator. Seven hundred miles a second and still accelerating! He felt suddenly tired and when Mado opened the door of a sleeping cabin its spotless bunk looked very inviting. He turned in without protest.

CHAPTER III

A Message

The days passed quickly, whether measured by the Martian chronometer aboard the *Nomad* or by Carr's watch, which he was regulating to match the slightly longer day of the red planet. He was becoming proficient in the operation of all mechanisms of the ship and had developed a fondness for its every appointment.

Behind them the sun was losing much of its blinding magnificence as it receded into the ebon background of the firmament. The Earth was but one of the countless worlds visible through the stern ports, distinguishable by its slightly greenish tinge. They had reached the vicinity of the phenomenon of space Mado had previously discovered. Carr found himself seething with excitement as the *Nomad* was brought to a drifting speed.

Mado, who had disclaimed all knowledge of navigation, was busy in the turret with a sextant. He made rapid calculations based on its indications and hurried to the controls.

"Find it?" Carr asked.

"Yep. Be there in a half hour."

The nose of the vessel swung around and Mado adjusted the gravity energy carefully. Carr glued his eye to the telescope.

"See anything?" inquired Mado.

"About a million stars, that's all."

"Funny. Should be close by."

Then: "Yes! Yes! I see it!" Carr exulted. "A milky cloud. Transparent almost. To the right a little more!"

The mysterious cloud rushed to meet them and soon was visible to the naked eye through the forward port. Their speed increased alarmingly and Mado cut off the energy.

"What's that?" Mado stared white-faced at his friend.

"A voice! You hear it too?"

"Yes. Listen!"

Amazed, they gazed at each other. It was a voice; yet not a sound came to their ears. The voice was in their own consciousness. A mental message! Yet each heard and understood. There were no words, but clear mental images.

"Beware!" it seemed to warn. "Come not closer, travelers from afar. There is danger in the milky fleece before you!"

Mado pulled frantically at the energy reverse control. The force was now fully repelling. Still the billowing whiteness drew nearer. It boiled and bubbled with the ferocity of one of the hot lava cauldrons of Mercury. Changing shape rapidly, it threw out long streamers that writhed and twisted like the arms of an octopus. Reaching. Searching for victims!

"God!" whispered Carr. "What is it?"

"Take warning," continued the voice that was not a voice. "A great ship, a royal ship from a world unknown to you, now is caught in the grip of this mighty monster. We can not escape, and death draws quickly near. But we can warn others and ask that our fate be reported to our home body."

A sudden upheaval of the monstrous mass spewed forth an object that bounced a moment on the rippling surface and then was lost to view. A sphere, glinting golden against the white of its awful captor.

"The space-ship!" gasped Mado. "It's vanished again!"

They hurtled madly in the direction of this monster of the heavens, their reverse energy useless.

"We're lost, Mado." Carr was calm now. This was excitement with a vengeance. He'd wished for it and here it was. But he'd much rather have a chance to fight for his life. Fine ending to his dreams!

"Imps of the canals! The thing's alive!" Mado hurled himself at the controls as a huge blob of the horrible whiteness broke loose from the main body and wobbled uncertainly toward them. A long feeler reached forth and grasped the errant portion, returning it with a vicious jerk.

"Turn back! Turn back!" came the eery warning from the golden sphere. "All is over for us. Our hull is crushed. The air is pouring from our last compartment. Already we find breathing difficult. Turn back! The third satellite of the fifth planet is our home. Visit it, we beseech you, and report the manner of our going. This vile creature of space has power to draw you to its breast, to crush you as we are crushed."

The *Nomad* lurched and shuddered, drawn ever closer to the horrid mass of the thing. A gigantic jellyfish, that's what it was, a hundred miles across! Carr shivered in disgust as it throbbed anew, sending out those grasping streamers of its mysterious material. As the *Nomad* plunged to its doom with increasing speed, Mado tried to locate some spot in the universe where an extreme effect could be obtained from the full force of the attracting or repulsive energies. They darted this way and that but always found themselves closer to the milky billows that now were pulsating in seeming eagerness to engulf the new victim.

Once more came the telepathic warning, "Delay no longer. It is high time you turned back. You must escape to warn our people and yours. Even now the awful creature has us in its vitals, its tentacles reaching through our shattered walls, creeping and twining through the passages of our vessel. Crushing floors and walls, its demoniac energies heating our compartment beyond belief. We can hold out no longer. Go! Go quickly. Remember—the third satellite of the fifth planet—to the city of golden domes. Tell of our fate. Our people will understand. You—"

The voice was stilled. Mado groaned as if in pain and Carr saw in that instant that each knob and lever on the control panel glowed with an unearthly brush discharge. Not violet as of high frequency electricity, but red. Cherry red as of heated metal. The emanations of the cosmic monster were at work on the *Nomad.* A glance through the forward port showed they had but a few miles to go. They'd be in the clutches of the horror in minutes, seconds, at the rate they were traveling. Mado slumped in his seat, his proud head rolling grotesquely on his breast. He slid to the floor, helpless.

Carr went mad with fury. It couldn't be! This thing of doom was a creature of his imagination! But no—there it was, looming close in his vision. By God, he'd leave the mark of the *Nomad* on the vicious thing! He remembered the ray with which the vessel was armed. He was in the pilot's seat, fingering controls that blistered his hands and cramped his arms with an unnameable force. He'd fight the brute! Full energy—head on—that was the way to meet it. Why bother with the reversal? It was no use.

A blood-red veil obscured his vision. He felt for the release of the ray; pulled the gravity energy control to full power forward. In a daze, groping blindly for support, he waited for the shock of impact. The mass of that monstrosity must be terrific, else why had it such a power of attraction for other bodies? Or was it that the thing radiated energies unknown to science? Whatever it was, the thing would know the sting of the *Nomad's* ray. Whatever its nature, animate or inanimate, it was matter. The ray destroyed matter. Obliterated it utterly. Tore the atoms asunder, whirling their electrons from their orbits with terrific velocity. There'd be some effect, that was certain! No great use perhaps. But a crater would mark the last resting place of the *Nomad*; a huge crater. Perhaps the misty whiteness would close in over them later. But there'd be less of the creature's bulk to menace other travelers in space.

His head ached miserably; his body was shot through and through with cramping agonies. The very blood in his veins was liquid fire, searing his veins and arteries with pulsing awfulness. He staggered from the control cabin; threw himself on his bunk. The covers were electrified and clung to him like tissue to rubbed amber. The wall of the sleeping cabin vibrated with a screeching note. The floors trembled. Madness! That's all it was! He'd awaken in a moment. Find himself in his own bed at home. He'd dreamed of adventures before now. But never of such as this! It just couldn't happen! A nightmare—fantasy of an over-tired brain—it was.

There came a violent wrench that must have torn the hull plates from their bracings. The ship seemed to close in on him and crush him. A terrific concussion flattened him to the bunk. Then all was still. Carr Parker's thoughts broke short abruptly. He had slipped into unconsciousness.

CHAPTER IV

Europa

When Carr opened his eyes it was to the normal lighting of his own sleeping cabin. The *Nomad* was intact, though an odor of scorched varnish permeated the air. They were unharmed—as yet. He turned on his side and saw that Mado was moving about at the side of his couch. Good old Mado! With a basin of water in his hand and a cloth. He'd been bathing his face. Brought him to. He sat up just as Mado turned to apply the cloth anew.

"Good boy, Carr! All right?" smiled the Martian.

"Little dizzy. But I'm okay." Carr sprang to his feet where he wabbled uncertainly for a moment. "But the *Nomad?*" he asked. "Is she—are we safe?"

"Never safer. What in the name of Saturn did you do?"

Carr passed his hand across his eyes, trying to remember. "The D-ray," he said. "I turned it on and dived into the thing with full attraction. Then—I forget. Where is it—the thing, I mean?"

"Look!" Mado drew him to the stern compartment.

Far behind them there shone a misty wreath, a ring of drifting matter that writhed and twisted as if in mortal agony.

"Is that it?"

"What's left of it. You shot your way through it; through and out of its influence. D-ray must have devitalized the thing as it bored through. Killed its energies—for the time, at least."

Already, the thing was closing in. Soon there would be a solid mass as before. But the *Nomad* was saved.

"How about yourself?" asked Carr anxiously. "Last time I saw you you were flat on the floor."

"Nothing wrong with me now. A bit stiff and sore, that's all. When I came to I put all the controls in neutral and came looking for you. I was scared, but the thing's all over now, so let's go."

"Where?"

"Europa."

"Where's that?"

"Don't you remember? The third satellite of the fifth planet. That's Europa, third in distance from Jupiter, the fifth planet. It is about the size of Terra's satellite—your Moon. We'll find the city of the golden domes."

Carr's eyes renewed their sparkle. "Right!" he exclaimed. "I forgot the mental message. Poor devils! All over for them now. But we'll carry their message. How far is it?"

"Don't know yet till I determine our position and the position of Jupiter. But it's quite a way. Jupiter's 483 million miles from the Sun, you know."

"We're more than half way, then."

"Not necessarily. Perhaps we're on the opposite side of the sun from Jupiter's present position. Then we'd have a real trip."

"Let's figure it out." Carr was anxious to be off.

Luck was with them, as they found after some observations from the turret. Jupiter lay off their original course by not more than fifteen degrees. It was but four days' journey.

Again they were on their way and the two men, Martian and Terrestrial, made good use of the time in renewing their old friendship and in the study of astronomy as they had done during the first leg of their journey. Though of widely differing build and nature, the two found a close bond in their similar inclinations. The library of the Nomad was an excellent one. Thrygis had seen to that, all of the voice-vision reels being recorded in Cos, the interplanetary language, with its standardized units of weight and measurement.

The supplies on board the *Nomad* were ample. Synthetic foods there were for at least a hundred Martian days. The supply of oxygen and water was inexhaustible, these essential items being produced in automatic retorts where disassembled electrons from their cosmic-ray hydrogen were reassembled in the proper structure to produce atoms of any desired element. Their supply of synthetic food could be replenished in like manner when necessity arose. Thrygis had forgotten nothing.

"How do you suppose we'll make ourselves understood to the people of Europa?" asked Carr, when they had swung around the great orb of Jupiter and were headed toward the satellite.

"Shouldn't have any trouble, Carr. Believe me, to a people who have progressed to the point of sending mental messages over five hundred miles of space, it'll be a cinch, understanding our simple mental processes. Bet they'll read our every thought."

"That's right. But the language. Proper names and all that. Can't get those over with thought waves."

"No, but I'll bet they'll have some way of solving that too. You wait and see."

Carr lighted a cigar and inhaled deeply as he gazed from one of the ports. He'd never felt better in his life. Always had liked Martian tobacco, too. Wondered what they'd do when the supply ran out. One thing they couldn't produce synthetically. The disc of the satellite loomed near and it shone with a warmly inviting light. Almost red, like the color of Mars, it was. Sort of golden, rather. Anyway, he wondered what awaited them there. This was a great life, this roaming in space, unhampered by laws or conventions. The *Nomad* was well named.

"Wonder what they'll think of our yarn," he said.

"And me. I wonder, too, what that ungodly thing was back there. The thing that is now the grave of some of their people. And what the golden sphere was doing so far from home. It's a mystery."

They had gone over the same ground a hundred times and had not reached a satisfactory conclusion. But perhaps they'd learn more in the city of golden domes.

"Another thing," said Carr, "that's puzzled me. Why is it that Europa has not been discovered before this; that it's inhabited, I mean?"

"Rocket ships couldn't carry enough fuel. Besides, our astronomers've always told us that the outer planets were too cold; too far from the sun."

"That is something to think about. Maybe we'll not be able to stand the low temperature; thin atmosphere; low surface gravity."

"We've our insulated suits and the oxygen helmets for the first two objections. The G-rays'll hold us down in any gravity. But we'll see mighty soon. We're here."

They had entered the atmosphere as they talked and the *Nomad* was approaching the surface in a long glide with repulsion full on. It was daytime on the side they neared. Pale daylight, but revealing. The great ball that was Jupiter hung low on the horizon, its misty outline faintly visible against the deep green of the sky.

The surface over which they skimmed was patchworked with farm-lands and crisscrossed by gleaming ribbons. Roadways! It was like the voice-vision records of the ancient days on Mars and Terra before their peoples had taken to the air. Here was a body where a person could get out in the open; next to nature. They crossed a lake of calm green water fringed by golden sands. At its far side a village spread out beneath them and was gone; a village of broad pavements and circular dwellings with flat rooms, each with its square of ground. A golden, mountain range loomed in the background; vanished beneath them. More fields and roads. Everywhere there were yellows and reds and the silver sheen of the roads. No green save that of the darkening sky and the waters of the streams and ponds. It was a most inviting panorama.

Occasionally they passed a vessel of the air—strange flapping-winged craft that soared and darted like huge birds. Once one of them approached so closely they could see its occupants, seemingly a people similar to the Venusians, small of stature and slender.

"How in time are we to find this city of golden domes?" Carr ejaculated.

As if in answer to his question there came a startling command, another of the mental messages.

"Halt!" it conveyed to their mind. "Continue not into our country until we have communed with you."

Obediently Mado brought up the nose of the *Nomad* and slowed her down to a gradual stop. They hovered at an altitude of about four thousand feet, both straining their ears as if listening for actual speech.

"It is well," continued the message. "Your thoughts are good. You come from afar seeking the city of golden domes. Proceed now and a fleet of our vessels will meet you and guide you to our city."

"Now wouldn't that jar you?" whispered Carr. "Just try to get away with anything on this world."

Mado laughed as he started the generators of the propelling energy. "I'd hate to have a wife of Europa," he commented. "No sitting-up-with-sick-friend story could get by with her!"

CHAPTER V

The City of Golden Domes

With the *Nomad* cruising slowly over the surface of the peaceful satellite, Mado sampled the atmosphere through a tube which was provided for that purpose. The pressure was low, as they had expected; about twenty inches of mercury in the altitude at which they drifted. But the oxygen content was fairly high and the impurities negligible. A strange element was somewhat in evidence, though Mado's analysis showed this to be present in but minute quantity. They opened the ports and drew their first breath of the atmosphere of Europa.

"Good air, Carr." Mado was sniffing at one of the ports. "A bit rare for you, but I think you'll get along with it. Temperature of forty-five degrees. That's not so bad. The strangest thing is the gravity. This body isn't much more than two thousand miles in diameter, yet its gravity is about the same as on Venus—seven eighths of that of Terra. Must have a huge nickel-iron core."

"Yes. It'll be a cinch for me. But you, you big lummox—it's the G-ray for you as long as we're here."

"Uh-huh. You get all the breaks, don't you?"

Carr laughed. He was becoming anxious to land. "What sort of a reception do you suppose we'll get?" he said.

"Not bad, from the tone of that last message. And here they come, Carr. Look—a dozen of them. A royal reception, so far."

Suddenly they were in the midst of a flock of great birds; birds that flapped their golden wings to rise, then soared and circled like the gulls of the terrestrial oceans. And these mechanical birds were fast. Carr and Mado watched in fascination as they strung out in V formation and led the way in the direction of the setting sun. Six, seven hundred miles an hour the *Nomad's* indicator showed, as they swung in behind these ships of Europa.

They crossed a large body of water, a lake of fully five hundred miles in width. More country then, hardly populated now and with but few of the gleaming roadways. The sun had set, but there was scarcely any diminution of the light for the great ball that was Jupiter reflected a brilliance of far greater intensity than that of the full Moon on a clear Terrestrial night. A marvelous sight the gigantic body presented, with its alternate belts of gray-blue and red and dazzling white. And it hung so low and huge in the heavens that it seemed one had but to stretch forth a hand to touch its bright surface.

Another mountain range loomed close and was gone. On its far side there stretched the desolate wastes of a desert, a barren plain that extended in all directions to the horizon. Wind-swept, it was and menacing beneath them. Europa was not all as they had first seen it.

A glimmer of brightness appeared at the horizon. The fleet was reducing speed and soon they saw that their journey was nearly over. At the far edge of the desert the bright spot resolved itself into the outlines of a city, the city of golden domes. Cones they looked like, rather, with rounded tops and fluted walls. The mental message had conveyed the most fitting description possible without words or picture.

The landing was over so quickly that they had but confused impressions of their reception. A great square in the heart of the city, crowded with people. Swooping maneuvers of hundreds of the bird-like ships. An open space for their arrival. The platform where a committee awaited them. The king, or at least he seemed to be king. The sea of upturned faces, staring eyes.

Mado fidgeted and opened his mouth to voice a protest but Carr nudged him into silence. The king had risen from his seat in the circle on the platform and was about to address them. There was no repetition of the telepathic means of communication.

"Welcome, travelers from the inner planets," said the king. He spoke Cos perfectly! "Cardos, emperor of the body you call Europa, salutes you. Our scientists have recorded your thoughts with their psycho-ray apparatus and have learned that you have a message for us, a message we fear is not pleasant. Am I correct?"

Carr stared at the soft-voiced monarch of this remarkable land. It was incredible that he spoke in the universal language of the inner planets!

"Your Highness," he replied, "is correct. We have a message. But it amazes us that you are familiar with our language."

"That we shall explain later. Meanwhile—the message!"

"The message," Carr said, "is not pleasant. A golden sphere out in space. Helpless in the clutches of a nameless monster, a vast creature of jellylike substance but possessed of enormous destructive energy. A mental message to our vessel warning us away and bidding us to come here; to tell you of their fate. We escaped and here we are."

The face of Cardos paled. He reached for an egg-shaped crystal that reposed on the table; spoke rapidly into its shimmering depths. Hidden amplifiers carried his voice throughout the square in booming tones. It was a strange tongue he spoke, with many gutturals and sibilants. A groan came up from the assembled multitude.

Cardos tossed the crystal to the table with a resigned gesture, then tottered and swayed. Instant confusion reigned in the square and the emperor was assisted from the platform by two of his retainers. They never saw him again.

One of the counsellors, a middle-aged man with graying russet hair and large gray eyes set in a perfectly smooth countenance, stepped from the platform and grasped the two adventurers as the confusion in the square increased to an uproar.

"Come," he whispered, in excellent Cos; "I'll explain all to you in the quiet of my own apartments. I am Detis, a scientist, and my home is close by."

Gently he clung to them as the larger men forced their way between the milling groups of excited Europans. No one gave them much attention. All seemed to be overcome with grief. A terrible disaster, this loss of the golden sphere must be!

They were out of the square and in one of the broad streets. The fluted sides of the unpointed cones shone softly golden on all sides. Alike in every respect were these dwellings of the people of Europa, and strangely attractive in the light of the mother planet.

Not a word was spoken when they reached the abode of their guide. They entered an elaborate hall and were whisked upward in an automatic elevator. Detis ushered them into his apartment when they alighted. He smiled gravely at their looks of wonder as they cast eyes on the maze of apparatus before them. It was a laboratory rather than a living room in which they stood.

Detis led them to an adjoining room where he bid them be seated. They exchanged wondering glances as their host paced the floor vigorously before speaking further.

"Friends," he finally blurted, "I hope you'll excuse my emotion but the news you brought is a terrible blow to me as to all Europa. Carli, our prince, beloved son of Cardos, was commander of the ship you reported lost. We deeply mourn his loss."

Carr and Mado waited in respectful silence while their host made effort to control his feelings.

"Now," he said, after a moment, "I can talk. You have many questions to ask, I know. So have I. But first I must tell you that Carli's was an expedition to your own worlds. A grave danger hangs over them and he was sent to warn them. He has been lost. Our only space-ship capable of making the journey also is lost. Six Martian years were required to build it, so I fear the warning will never reach your people. Already the time draws near."

"A grave danger?" asked Mado. "What sort of a danger?"

"War! Utter destruction! Conquest by the most warlike and ambitious people in the solar system."

"Not the people of Europa?" asked Carr.

"Indeed not. There is another inhabited satellite of Jupiter, next farthest from the mother planet. Ganymede, you call it. It is from there that these conquerors are to set forth."

"Many of them?" inquired Mado.

"Two million or so. They're prepared to send an army of more than a tenth of that number on the first expedition."

"A mere handful!" Carr was contemptuous.

"True, but they are armed with the most terrible of weapons. Your people are utterly unprepared and, unless warned, will be driven from their cities and left in the deserts to perish of hunger and exposure. This is a real danger."

"Something in it, Carr, if what he says is true. We've no arms nor warriors. Haven't had for two centuries. You know it as well as I do."

"Bah! Overnight we could have a million armed and ready to fight them off."

Detis raised his hand. "You offend me," he said gravely. "I have told you this in good faith and you reward me with disbelief and boastful talk. Your enemies are more powerful than you think, and your own people utterly defenceless against them."

"I'm sorry," Carr apologized, "and I'll listen to all you have to say. Surely your prince has not given his life in vain." He was ashamed before this scientist of Europa.

A tinkling feminine voice from the next room called something in the Europan tongue.

Detis raised his head proudly and his frown softened at the sound of dainty footsteps. His voice was a caress as he replied.

A vision of feminine loveliness stood framed in the doorway and the visitors rose hastily from their seats. Carr gazed into eyes of the deepest blue he had ever seen. Small in stature though this girl of Europa was—not more than five feet tall—she had the form of a goddess and the face of an angel. He was flushing to the roots of his hair. Could feel it spread. What an ass he was anyway! Anyone'd think he'd never seen a woman in all his thirty-five years!

"My daughter, Ora, gentlemen," said Detis.

The girl's eyes had widened as she looked at the huge Martian with the funny black box on his back. They dropped demurely when turned to those of the handsome Terrestrial.

"Oh," she said, in Cos, "I didn't know you had callers."

CHAPTER VI

Vlor-urdin

The time passed quickly in Pala-dar, city of the golden domes. Detis spent many hours in the laboratory with his two visitors and the fair Ora was usually at his side. She was an efficient helper to her father and a gracious hostess to the guests.

The amazement of the visitors grew apace as the wonders of Europan science were revealed to them. They sat by the hour at the illuminated screen of the rulden, that remarkable astronomical instrument which brought the surfaces of distant celestial bodies within a few feet of their eyes, and the sounds of the streets and the jungles to their ears. It was no longer a mystery how the language of Cos had become so familiar to these people.

They learned of the origin of the races that inhabited Europa and Ganymede. Ages before, it was necessary for the peoples of the then thickly populated Jupiter to cast about for new homes due to the cooling of the surface of that planet. Life was becoming unbearable. In those days there were two dominant races on the mother body, a gentle and peaceful people of great scientific accomplishment and a race of savage brutes who, while very clever with their hands, were of lesser mental strength and of a quarrelsome and fighting disposition.

Toward the last the population of both main countries was reduced to but a few survivors, and the intelligent race had discovered a means of traversing space and was prepared to leave the planet for the more livable satellite—Europa. Learning of these plans, the others made a treaty of perpetual peace as a price for their passage to another satellite—Ganymede. The migration began and the two satellites were settled by the separate bands of pioneers and their new lives begun.

The perpetual treaty had not been broken since, but the energies of the warlike descendants of those first settlers of Ganymede were expended in casting about for new fields to conquer. Through the ages they cast increasingly covetous eyes on those inner planets, Mars, Terra and Venus. Not having the advantage of the Rulden, they knew of these bodies only what could be seen through their own crude optical instruments and what they had learned by word of mouth from certain renegade Europans they were able to bribe.

While their neighbors of the smaller satellite were engaged in peaceful pursuits, tilling the soil and making excellent homes for themselves, the dwellers on Ganymede were fashioning instruments of warfare and building a fleet of space-ships to carry them to their intended victims. It was a religion with them; they could think of nothing else. An unscrupulous scientist of Europa sold himself to them several generations previously and it was this scientist who had made the plans for their space-fliers and had contrived the deadly weapons with which they were armed. He likewise taught them the language of Cos and it now was spoken universally throughout Ganymede in anticipation of the glorious days of conquest.

"You honestly believe them able to do this?" asked Carr, still skeptical after two days of discussion.

"I know it as a certainty," Detis replied solemnly. "It is only during the past generation we have learned of the completeness and awfulness of their preparations. Your people can not combat their sound-ray. With it they can remain outside the vision of those on the surface and set the tall buildings of your cities in harmonic vibrations that will bring them down in ruins about the ears of the populace."

"There'll be nothing left for them to take if they destroy all our cities: nowhere for them to live. I don't get it."

"Only a few will be destroyed completely, to terrify the rest of the inhabitants of your worlds. Others will be depopulated by means of vibrations that will kill off the citizens without harming the cities themselves—vibrations which are capable of blanketing a large area and raising the body temperature of all living things therein to a point where death will ensue in a very few minutes. Other vibrations will paralyze all electrical equipment on the planet and make it impossible for your ships of the air to set out to give battle, even were they properly armed."

"Looks bad, Carr," said Mado glumly.

"It does that. We've got to go back and carry the warning."

"I fear it is too late," said Detis. "Much time will be needed in which to develop a defense and surely it can not be done within the three isini before they set forth—about four of your days."

"They leave that soon?" Carr was taken aback.

"Yes, with their one hundred and twenty vessels; forty to each of your three planets; seventeen hundred men to a vessel."

Carr jumped to his feet. "By the heat devils of Mercury!" he roared, "well go to their lousy little satellite and find a way to prevent it!"

Ora gazed at his flushed face with unconcealed admiration.

"You're crazy!" exploded Mado. "What can we do with the *Nomad*?"

"Her D-ray can do plenty of damage."

"Yes, but they'd have us down before we could account for five of their vessels. It's no use, I tell you."

But Carr was stubborn. "We'll pay them a call anyway. I'll bet we can dope out some way of putting it over on them. Are you game?"

"Of course I'm game. I'll go anywhere you will. But it's a fool idea just the same."

"Maybe so. Maybe not. Anyway—let's go."

"Just a moment, gentlemen," Detis interposed. "How about me?"

Carr stared at him and saw that his eyes shone with excitement. "Why, I believe you'd like to go with us!" he exclaimed admiringly.

"I would, indeed."

"Come on then. We're off." He was impatient to be gone.

Detis busied himself with a small apparatus that folded into a compact case, explaining that it was one that might prove useful. Ora left the room but quickly returned. She too carried a small case, and she had donned a snug fitting leather garment that covered her from neck to knees.

"What's this?" demanded Carr. "Surely Miss Ora does not intend to come with us?"

"She never leaves my side," said Detis proudly.

"Nothing doing!" Carr stated emphatically. "There'll be plenty of danger on this trip. Well have no woman along—least of all your charming daughter."

Mado was leaving everything to his friend, but he grinned in anticipation when he saw the look of anger on the girl's face.

She stamped her little foot and faced Carr valiantly. "See here, Mr. Carr Parker!" she stormed. "I'm no weakling. I'm the daughter of my father and where he goes I go. You'll take me or I'll never speak to you again."

Carr flushed. He was accustomed to his own way in most things and entirely unused to the ways of the gentler sex. He could have shaken the little vixen! But now she was standing before him and there was something in those great blue eyes besides anger; something that set his heart pounding madly.

"All right!" he agreed desperately, "have your own way."

He turned on his heel and strode to the door. Giving in to this slip of a girl! What a fool he was! But it would be great at that to have her along in the *Nomad.*

They found the public square deserted, the gilded dwellings hung with somber colors in mourning for Carli. Ora and Detis were very quiet and preoccupied when they entered the *Nomad.* The five isini of lamentation for the young prince had not yet passed.

The two Europans were delighted with the appointments and mechanisms of the little vessel from Mars. They investigated every nook and cranny of its interior during the journey and were voluble in their praise of its inventor and builder. Neither had ever set foot in a space-flier and each was seized with a longing to explore space with these two strangers from the inner planets. They would make a couple of good vagabonds along with Mado and himself, Carr thought as they expressed their feelings. But there was more serious business at hand. They were nearing Ganymede.

"Where'll we land, Detis?" Mado called from the control cabin.

"Vlor-urdin. That is their chief city. I'll guide you to the location."

They took up their places at the ports and scanned the surface of the satellite as Mado dropped the ship into its atmosphere. A far different scene was presented than on Europa. The land was seamed and scarred, the colors of the foliage somber. Grays and browns predominated and the jungles seemed impenetrable. A river swung into view and its waters were black as the deepest night, its flow sluggish. A rank mist hung over the surface.

"The river of Charis!" exclaimed Detis. "Follow it, Mado. No, the other direction. There! It leads directly to Vlor-urdin."

By good chance they had entered the atmosphere at a point not far from their destination. In less than an hour by the *Nomad's* chronometer the towers of Vlor-urdin were sighted.

It was a larger city than Pala-dar and of vastly different appearance. A hollow square of squat buildings enclosed the vast workshops and storage space of the fleet of war vessels. Their huge spherical bulks rose from their cradles in tier after tier that stretched as far as the eye could reach when the *Nomad* had dropped to a level but slightly above the tips of the highest spires. The spires were everywhere, decorative towers at the corners of the squat buildings. Everything was black, the vessels of the fleet, the squat buildings and the spires of Vlor-urdin. Death was in the air. Rank vapor drifted in through the opened ports. There was silence in the city below them and silence in the *Nomad.*

Ora shuddered and drew closer to him. Carr was aware of her nearness and a lump rose in his throat. A horrible fear assailed him. Fear for the safety of the dainty Europan at his side. He found her hand; covered it protectingly with his own.

CHAPTER VII

Rapaju

Detis was setting up and adjusting the complicated mechanisms of his little black case. A dozen vacuum tubes lighted, and a murmur of throbbing energy came from a helix of shining metallic ribbon that topped the whole. Flexible cables led to a cap-like contrivance which Detis placed on his head. He frowned in concentration.

"The psycho-ray apparatus." Ora explained. "He's sending a message to the city."

Evidently the influence of the ray was directive. They had no inkling of the thoughts transmitted from the alert brain of the scientist but, from the look of satisfaction on his face, they could see that he was obtaining the desired contact.

"Rapaju," he exclaimed, switching off the power of his instrument, "commander of the fleet of the Llotta. I have advised him of our arrival. Told him that a Martian and a Terrestrial wish to treat with him concerning the proposed invasion of their planets. His answering thought first was of fiercest rage, then conciliatory in nature. He'll receive you and listen to your arguments, though he promises nothing. Is that satisfactory?"

"Yes." Carr and Mado were agreed. At least it would give them a chance to look over the ground and to make plans, should any occur to them.

The *Nomad* circled over the heart of the city and soon Mado saw a suitable landing space. They settled gracefully in an open area close by the building indicated by Detis as that of the administration officials of the city.

A group of squat, sullen Llotta awaited them and, without speaking a word either of hatred or welcome, led them into the forbidding entrance of the building. Close-set, beady eyes; unbelievably flat features of chalky whiteness; chunky bowed legs, bare and hairy; long arms with huge dangling paws—these were the outstanding characteristics of the Llotta. Mado stared straight before him, refusing to display any great interest in the loathsome creatures, but Carr was frankly curious and as frankly disapproving.

Rapaju leered maliciously when the four voyagers stood before him. He looked the incarnation of all that was evil and vile, a monster among monsters. Sensing him to be the more aggressive of the two visitors from doomed planets, he addressed his remarks to Carr.

"You come to plead with Rapaju," he sneered, his Cos tinged with an outlandish accent, "to beg for the worthless lives of your compatriots; for the wealth of your cities?"

"We come to reason with you," replied Carr haughtily, "if you are capable of reasoning. What is this incredible thing you are planning?"

Mado gasped at the effrontery of his friend. But Carr was oblivious of the warning looks cast in his direction.

"Enough of that!" snapped Rapaju. "I'll do the talking—you the reasoning. I've a proposition to make to you, and if you know what's best, you'll agree. Otherwise you'll be first of the Terrestrials to die. Is that clear?"

"Clear enough, all right," growled Carr. "What do you mean—a proposition?"

"Ha! I thought you'd listen. My offer is the lives of you and your companion in exchange for your assistance in guiding my fleet to the capital cities of your countries. Not that our plans will be changed if you refuse, but that much time will be saved in this manner and quick victory made certain without undue sacrifice of valuable property."

"You—you—!" Carr stammered in anger. But there was no use in raising a rumpus—now. They'd only kill him. Something might be accomplished if he pretended to accede. "Go on with your story," he finished lamely.

"In addition to sparing your lives I'll place you both in high position after we seize your respective planets. Make you chief officers in the prison lands we intend to establish for your countrymen. What do you say?"

"Will you give us time to talk it over and think about it?"

"Until the hour of departure, if you wish."

Carr bowed, avoiding Mado's questioning eyes. He looked at Ora where she stood at the side of Detis. She flashed him a guarded smile. He knew that she understood.

Rapaju relaxed. He was confident he could bribe these puerile foreigners to help him in the great venture. And sadly he needed such help. The Llotta were not navigators. Their knowledge of the heavens was sadly incomplete. They had no maps of the surfaces of the planets to be visited. Their simultaneous blows would be far more effective and the campaign much shorter if they could choose the most vital centers for the initial attacks.

"Now," he said, "that we understand one another, let us talk further of the plans. Then you will be able to consider carefully before making your decision."

Rapaju could be diplomatic when he wished. Carr longed to sink his fingers in the hairy throat. But he smiled hypocritically and found an opportunity to wink meaningly at Mado. This was going to be good! And who knew?—perhaps they might find some way to outwit these mad savages. To think of them in control of the inner planets was revolting.

They retired to a small room with Rapaju and four of his lieutenants, Detis and Ora accompanying them. Ora sat close to Carr at the circular table in Rapaju's council. Carr thought grimly of the board meetings in far away New York.

Rapaju talked. He told of the armament of his vessels, painting vivid pictures of the destruction to be wrought in the cities of Terra, of Mars and Venus. His great hairy paws clutched at imaginary riches when he spoke glowingly of the plundering to follow. He spoke of the women of the inner planets and Carr half rose from his seat when he observed the lecherous glitter in his beady eyes. Ora! Great God, was she safe here? He stole a glance at the girl and a recurrence of the awful fear surged through him. In her leather garment, close fitting and severe, she looked like a boy. Perhaps they would not know. Besides, there was the perpetual treaty with Europa. It always had been observed, Detis said.

As Rapaju expanded upon the glories to come he told perforce of many of the details of the plans. One thing stood out in Carr's mind: the vessels of the Llotta were not equal to the *Nomad* in many respects. They must carry their entire supply of fuel from the starting point and this was calculated as but a small percentage in excess of that required to carry them to their destinations. Their speed was not as great as the *Nomad's* by at least a third. If the *Nomad* led the fleet from Ganymede they might be able to get them off their course; cause them to run out of fuel out in the vacuum and absolute zero of space. He kicked Mado under the table and arose to ask a few leading questions.

Ora was whispering to her father and he nodded his head as if in complete agreement with what she was saying. These two were not deceived by his apparent traitorous talk, but Mado was aghast. Carr wondered if Rapaju believed him as did his friend.

"We'll do it, Rapaju," he stated finally. "In our ship, the *Nomad*, we'll guide you across the trackless wastes of the heavens. We'll take you to our capital cities; point out to you the richest of the industrial centers. We have no love for our own worlds. Mado and I deserted them for a life of vagabondage amongst the stars. We ask no reward other than that we be permitted to leave once more on our travels, to roam space as we choose."

Mado attempted to voice an objection but Carr's hand was heavy on his shoulder. "Shut up, you fool!" he hissed in his ear. "Can't you trust me?"

Rapaju's eyes seemed to draw closer together as he returned Carr's unflinching stare. He walked around the table and stood at the side of the tall Terrestrial. Suddenly he grasped Ora's jacket, tore it open at the throat. He ran his hairy fingers over the bare shoulder of the shrinking girl and gurgled his delight at the velvet smoothness of her skin.

With a roar like a wild animal Carr was upon him, bearing him to the floor. His fingers were in that hairy throat, where they had itched to twine.

"Dirty, filthy beast!" he was snarling. "Lay your foul hands on Ora, will you? Say your prayers, if you know any, you swine!"

Then his muscles went limp and he was jerked to his feet by a terrible force, a force that sent him reeling and gasping against the wall. One of Rapaju's lieutenants stood before him with a tiny weapon in his hand, the weapon which had released the paralyzing gas he breathed. He was choking; suffocating. A black mist rose before him. He felt his knees give way. Dimly, as in a dream, he saw that Ora was in Detis' arms. Rapaju was on his feet, fingering his neck and laughing horribly.

"The treaty, Rapaju!" Detis was shouting.

Ora was sobbing. Mado was in the hands of two of the vile Llotta, struggling wildly to free himself. The Martian's eyes accused him. He shut his own and groaned. Opened them again. But it was no use. Everything in the room was whirling now, crazily. He fought to regain his senses, crawled weakly toward the squat figure of Rapaju where it swayed and twisted and spun around. Then all was darkness. The gas had taken its toll.

CHAPTER VIII

The Expedition

Carr awakened to a sense of wordless disgust. Fool that he was to spill the beans as he had! All set to put one over on the leader of the Llotta, then to come a cropper like this! He knew he had been spared for a purpose. The gas was not intended to kill, only to render him helpless for a time. He opened his eyes to the light of a familiar room. He had awakened before in this bed. It was his own cabin on board the *Nomad.* What had happened?

Had he dreamed it all. Europa, Ora, Rapaju—all of it? He sat up and felt of his aching head.

"Oh, are you awake?" a soft voice greeted him.

"Ora!" he exclaimed. It was indeed she, beautiful as ever.

"Sh-h," she warned, placing the tip of a finger to his lips. "They'll hear us."

"Who?" he whispered.

"Rapaju—his two guards. They're in the control cabin with father and Mado."

"What? They've taken the *Nomad*?"

"Yes. We're under way. They've forced Mado to guide them but do not trust him. Rapaju spared you as he believes you more capable. He'll hold you to your word."

"Lord! But what are you doing here?"

Ora dropped her eyes. "He—Rapaju—" she said, "inferred from your action in assaulting him that you were very fond of me. He holds me as a hostage for your good behavior. Father volunteered to come along. He persuaded Rapaju to allow it. Swore allegiance to his cause. Of course he wouldn't leave me."

Carr gazed at her in admiration of her courage. She had been nursing him, too! What a girl she was!

"Ora," he said huskily, "Rapaju was right. I am fond of you. More than fond: I love you. I never knew I could feel this way."

"Oh Carr, you mustn't!" She drew back as he scrambled to his feet. "They'll find us. We must not show that we care. Rapaju is a beast. He wants me for himself and is delaying the time only until you have brought the fleet safely to the inner planets and to their great cities. He—"

"The skunk! Wants you himself, does he? Why, why didn't I kill him? But Ora, you said—you do care—"

"Ha! I thought so!" Rapaju stood in the doorway, grinning mockingly at the pair. "The impetuous Terrestrial is up and about. Back at his old game!"

"Please, please, for my sake, Carr!" Ora pressed him back as he tensed his muscles for a spring.

"Sorry I was so slow," Carr grated, over her shoulder. "Another five seconds, Rapaju, and I'd have had your windpipe out by the roots."

Rapaju scowled darkly and fingered his throat. "But, my dear Carr, you were too slow," he said, "and I live—and shall live—while you shall die. Meanwhile you'll carry out your agreement. Come, Ora."

The girl hesitated a moment, then with a pleading glance at Carr stepped from the room.

"All right now, Parker," snapped Rapaju. "Into your clothes and into the pilot's seat. You'll stay there, too, till the journey's over. Get busy!"

One of his guards had appeared in the doorway. Carr knew that resistance was useless. Besides, seated at those controls, he might think of something. Rapaju'd never get Ora if he could help it!

Mado's shoulders drooped and his face was haggard and drawn, but he summoned a smile when he saw Carr.

"Hello, Carr," he said. "You all right?"

"Sure. Rapaju says I've got to take the controls."

"Very well." Mado shrugged his broad shoulders and slipped from the pilot's seat. Two ugly Llotta guards were watching, ray-pistols in hand. "The chart is corrected, Carr, and—"

"Never mind the conversation!" Rapaju snarled. "There'll be no talk between you at all. Beat it to your cabin, Mado."

The Martian glowered and made as if to retort hotly.

"But Rapaju," Detis interposed, speaking from his position at one of the ports, "they'll have to consult regarding the course of the vessel. Mado is more familiar than Carr with the navigation of space."

"Shut up!" roared Rapaju. "I know what I am doing. And, what's more, you'll not converse with them, either! I'm running this expedition, and I'm not taking any chances."

Detis subsided and followed Mado through the passage to the sleeping cabins.

The ensuing silence was ominous. Carr could feel the eyes of the Llotta upon him as he examined the adjustments of the controls and peeped through the telescope. A glance at the velocity indicator showed him they were traveling at a rate of eight hundred miles a second. He studied the chart and soon made out their position. Jupiter was a hundred million miles behind them and they were heading almost due sunward. The automatic control mechanism was not functioning. Evidently Mado had kept this a secret—and for a purpose. He wished he could talk with his friend. They'd plan something.

"Like your job?" Rapaju was gloating over this Terrestrial who had dared to lay hands upon him.

"Yes, but not the company." Carr was disdainful.

"You'll like it less before I've finished with you. And get this straight. You think we're dependent on you to guide us to the inner planets, and that we'll not harm any of you until they are reached. Don't fool yourself! I've watched Mado and I've spent much time in the excellent library of the *Nomad*. I've learned plenty about the navigation of space and can reach those planets as quickly and directly as you. But it pleases me to see you work, so work you shall. I'll check you carefully, and don't think you can deceive me. Don't try to depart from the true course. The sun is my check as it is yours, and I'll keep constant tab on our position. Get it?"

"A rather long speech, Rapaju." Carr grinned into the evil face of the commander.

"Still defiant, eh? Suits me, Carr Parker. We'll have some nice talks here, and then—when it pleases me—you'll suffer. You shall live to see your home city crash in utter ruin; your people slain, starved, beaten. And, above all, there's Ora—"

"Don't defile her name in your ugly mouth, you—!"

Carr bit his tongue to keep back the torrent of invectives that sprang to his lips. This would never do! He'd get himself bumped off before they were well started. And while there was life there was hope. He'd stick to his guns and think; think and plan. If only he could have a few words with Mado. They must get out of this mess. There must be a way! There must!

Rapaju was laughing in triumph. Thought he had cowed him, did he? Boastful savage! If he could navigate the *Nomad* himself, why didn't he? Liar! He and Mado were godsends to him, and he knew it! His speech at the council table had been the real truth.

Foreign thoughts entered his mind. Detis, good old Detis, was using his thought apparatus in his own cabin! He paid no attention to the words of Rapaju when he left the control room. Detis was on the job! Between them they'd outwit this devil of Ganymede.

"Keep your courage," came the message. "I've read the thoughts of Mado and he bids you examine the chart carefully. He's made some notations in the ancient language of Mars. The automatic control of the *Nomad* can be used when necessary. He has not advised Rapaju of its existence."

Carr was encouraged and he concentrated on a suitable reply. But, though he did not consciously will it, his thoughts were of Ora.

Instantly there came the reassurance of her father. "Ora is not in immediate danger. Rapaju is saving her for his revenge on you. And I'm watching her constantly. A ray-pistol is concealed in my clothing, its charge ready for the foul creature in case he should lay hands on her. But you must plan an escape, and salvation for your worlds. Examine the chart at once."

He looked from the corner of his eye and saw that one of the Llotta guards was watching intently. He peered into the eye-piece of the telescope; made an inconsequential change in one of the adjustments. The guard stirred but did not arise. He looked at the chart with new interest, scanned its markings carefully. What had Mado marked for his attention? There were hundreds of notations, some in Cos and a few in the ancient Martian, all in Mado's painstaking chirography.

Ah, there it was! A tiny spot almost on their course, with Mado's minute notation. Sargasso Sea! What did it mean? Did Mado intend to lead the fleet into the embrace of that dreadful monster they had so fortunately escaped? An excellent idea to save the inner planets. But suicide for them! He'd do it though, if it weren't for Ora. She was so sweet and innocent. She must not die; must not suffer. Another way must be found. He groaned aloud as he realized that her predicament was the result of his own bullheadedness. If only he hadn't insisted on the trip to Ganymede. But then there was the problem of preserving the civilization of the inner planets. It had to be met.

There was a commotion behind him; a feminine shriek from the after cabins; loud shoutings from the beast called Rapaju. Carr's heart skipped a beat. He was paralyzed with fear. But only for an instant. With a bellow of rage he whirled around and started for the door, charging the two guards with head down and arms flailing.

CHAPTER IX

Nemesis

The Llotta did not use their ray-pistols. They were too busy attempting to elude the mad rushes of the powerful Terrestrial. Besides, there were good reasons they should not kill him—yet. Carr drove one of them halfway down the passageway with a well-planted punch. The other was on his back, hairy legs twined around his waist, an arm under his chin, drawing his head back with a steady and terrible pressure. He whirled around, trying to shake off his beastly antagonist.

But these powerful legs and arms held fast. He tore at the hairy ankles where they crossed in the pit of his stomach; wrenched them free. Still the creature clung to him, twisting his head until it seemed his neck must break. He found a waving foot with his right hand; wrenched it mightily. There was a sharp snap and the foot dangled limp in his fingers. He had broken the ankle. With a howl of pain his assailant let go and dropped to the floor to crawl away like a whipped cur.

In a flash Carr saw that the brute was reaching for his ray-pistol where it had dropped during the encounter. He kicked it from the reach of that hairy paw and sprang after it. With one of those little weapons in his hands the odds would change! His fingers closed on its grip just as Ora rushed into the room, closely followed by Rapaju, whose distorted features were terrible to behold. The cabin was full of them now; the guard he had first knocked down; the lust-crazed commander—the one with the broken ankle. All but Detis and Mado. Carr faced them alone.

So close was Rapaju to the girl that he dared not use the pistol, and now the uninjured guard was circling him, trying to get in a position where he could use his ray-pistol without endangering his commander. Carr fumbled for the release of the weapon he held in his hand; found it. The guard threw himself to the floor when he saw it raised; shouted a warning. But it was too late. The deadly ray had sped on its mission of death; struck him full in the middle. The twisted body lay still a moment and then collapsed like a punctured balloon, leaving his scant clothing in a limp heap—empty. A worthy miniature of the D-ray, this little weapon!

He turned to face Rapaju and saw that he was shielding himself with Ora's body. She had fainted and now hung drooping in the arms of the beast. Where was Mado? Detis? Good God—he'd killed them! Carr thought of that little spot on the chart. Must be very close now. They'd pass so near there'd be no escape. But he could not reach the controls without taking his eyes from Rapaju. That would have to wait.

Rapaju was backing toward the door, still holding the limp figure of the girl before him. The injured guard lay moaning on the floor.

"Drop her, you devil!" Carr shouted desperately as he saw that Rapaju soon would reach the passageway.

Then suddenly he reached for the controls and pushed the energy lever to full speed forward. He braced himself for the shock of acceleration and saw

Rapaju and Ora thrown backward into the passageway, the girl's body cushioned by that of her captor as they were flung violently to the floor. Madly he rushed to the narrow entrance and tore at the hairy arms that encircled the slender waist of the girl. He jerked the snarling commander of the Llotta expedition to his feet and slammed him against the metal wall.

"Now, you damn pig," he grunted, "I'll finish the job. Dirty scum of a rotten world!"

He dragged his victim into the control cabin and threw him to the floor. But Rapaju was like an eel. He wriggled from under him and snatched from the heap of clothing the ray-pistol of the disintegrated guard. With a yelp of triumph he rose to his knees and leveled the weapon.

A well placed kick sent it spinning and Carr was upon him. He snapped back the head with a terrible punch; then lifted the dazed creature to his feet and stepped back.

"Stand up and take it like a man!" he roared.

Rapaju shook his head to clear it and rushed in with a bellow of rage. Just what Carr wanted! Starting almost from the floor, his right came up to meet the vicious jaw with a crack that told of the terrific power behind it. Lifted from his feet and hurled half way across the room by the impact, Rapaju lay motionless where he fell.

Carr was at the telescope. Their speed was close to fifteen hundred miles a second. The monstrous mass of Mado's Sargasso Sea loomed close in his vision. Off their course by a hundred miles or more. They'd miss it all right. He had the situation in hand now on board the *Nomad.* But how about the fleet behind them? He thought fast and furiously. Another two minutes and they'd pass the thing; the inexplicable horror which had accounted for the golden sphere of the Europans. Could he use it? Suppose the fleet of the enemy—

The idea was full of possibilities.

He rushed to the stern compartment, and scanned the heavens for the massed body of spheres he knew would be the fleet of the Llotta. At this speed they must have fallen far behind. Yes, there they were. Not so far behind at that. The battle in the control room must have been a shorter one than it had seemed. He returned quickly to the controls and reversed the energy, to give the fleet a chance to catch up to him.

Closer came that mass of whitish jelly. And now it was much larger than before. The terrible creature, for living matter it was, beyond doubt, was growing with the rapidity of a rising flood. Great tentacles of its horrid translucent substance reached in all directions for possible victims. He sickened at the sight. But what a fate for the fleet of the Llotta! If only he could maneuver them into its influence.

He changed his course slightly and headed directly for the monster, again increasing speed. Perhaps—if he calculated the forces correctly—he could dive through it again with the D-ray to clear a path. But no. It was a miracle they had escaped before, and now the vicious thing was more than double its previous size. Once more he altered his course. He'd cross in front of the thing; skim it as close as he dared and shoot from its influence on the far side. The greater mass of the enemy vessels and their lack of a quick-acting repulsive force would prove their undoing.

Full speed ahead. A rapid mental calculation—an educated guess, rather—and he set the automatic control. Turning around to start for the stern compartment, he saw that Ora had recovered from her swoon and now stood swaying weakly in the passageway.

"Ora!" he exclaimed delightedly. He rushed to her side and supported her in a tender embrace.

"Rapaju?" she questioned with horror in her eyes.

"Won't bother you for a while, dear. But your father—Mado?"

"He gassed them. They'll recover." The brave girl had regained her composure.

"Good! But, come! Time's short." He half carried her to the rear, berating himself the while for his inability to pay her closer attention. With arms still around her he placed her at one of the stern ports.

"What is it, Carr?" She sensed his excitement.

"The fleet—see! We'll destroy them."

The spherical vessels were close behind, huddled together in mass formation and following the *Nomad* blindly.

"How, Carr?"

"Lead them into it. Wait tall you see! There's a—"

The *Nomad* lurched, and changed direction. Cold fear clutched at his throat. That devil of a guard! Why hadn't he killed him? He dashed through the passage, Ora at his heels.

Sure enough, the crippled guard had dragged himself to the controls; was manipulating the energy director as he had seen Mado do. They were heading directly for the terrible monster of the heavens!

No need now to peer through the telescope. The thing was visible to the naked eye. No power could save them! Carr hurled himself at the guard and tore at the hairy paw which gripped the lever. The throbbing of strange energies filled the air of the room, and Carr's brain pulsed with the maddening rhythm. The red discharge appeared at the projections of the control panels. He forgot the fleet of the Llotta, forgot the menace to his own world. Only Ora mattered now, and he had not the power to save her!

As in a daze he knew he was wrenching mightily at the body of the powerful minion of Rapaju. His fingers encountered heated metal—one of the ray-pistols. He felt the intense vibration of the weapon as its charge was released. But he still lived. The beast who held it had missed! Dimly he was conscious of the screams of Ora; of the yielding of the creature who fought him. An animal cry registered on his consciousness and he shook the suddenly limp Llotta from him. He knew somehow that his last enemy was gone.

A quick glance showed him that Ora was still on her feet, braced against the wall. The red veil was before his eyes. He grasped the controls, and fought desperately to keep his strength and senses. A streamer of horrid whiteness swung across his vision; slithered clammily over the glass of one of the forward ports. They were into the thing! It was the end! He groaned aloud as he fumbled with the mechanisms and strove to formulate a plan of escape.

The fleet, he knew, was just behind. An enormous mass. The repulsive energy astern would be terrific. He turned it full on. The whiteness obscured his vision. Then it was gone once more. A single streamer waved before him and encompassed them. The movement of these members must be inconceivably rapid, else they'd be invisible at the speed the *Nomad* was traveling. Full speed ahead. The repulsion full on in the direction of the center of the mass as well as astern. The framework of the *Nomad* creaked protestingly from the terrific forces that tore at her vitals.

Then suddenly they were released. The *Nomad* was shooting off into space. The resultant of those combined forces had done the trick. Only the edge of that devil-fish of space, had they touched. Free—they were free of the monster! The red veil lifted. He rushed to Ora's side. She was kneeling at one of the floor ports, breathing heavily but unharmed.

Below them they saw the swiftly receding mass: the fleet of the Llotta diving headlong, drawn inexorably into the rapacious embrace of the vile creature of the heavens. An instant the awful whiteness of the thing closed in greedily about the many spheres of the fleet; swallowed them from sight and contorted madly and with seeming glee over the triumph. Then, in a burst of blinding incandescence, it was gone. The monster, the fleet—everything—blasted into nothingness. The fuel storage compartments of the vessels of Ganymede had exploded! The heavens were rid of the inexplicable growing menace; the inner planets were saved from a terrible invasion. And the *Nomad* was safe. Ora, Detis, Mado—all were safe!

At his side Ora was trembling. Gently he raised her to her feet, and took her into his arms.

CHAPTER X

Vagabonds All

Together they cared for Detis and Mado; made them comfortable in their bunks until the time when the effects of the gas would wear off. Lucky it was that Rapaju had used the gas pistol rather than the ray. Perhaps it had been a mistake. Or perhaps he had needed the scientific knowledge of Detis, the familiarity with the inner planets that was Mado's. At any rate, they had no delusions regarding his designs on Ora or his hatred of Carr. By his own passions had the commander of the fleet been led to the error that cost him his life and made possible the destruction of his fleet.

Carr was torn by conflicting emotions. The delectable little Europan was most disturbing. He'd never had much use for the other sex—on Earth. Too dominating, most of them. And always thrown at his head by designing parents for his money. But Ora was different! Her very nearness set his pulses racing. And he knew that she cared for him as he did for her. Those moments in the control cabin after the explosion! But something had come over him since he cut loose from the old life. Wanderlust—that was it. He'd never go back. Neither would he be content to settle down to a domestic life in Paladar. Wanted to be up and going somewhere.

"Oh, Carr, Carr!" Ora's voice called to him. "Mado is awake. He wants you."

Good old Mado! Why couldn't they just continue on their way as they had started out? Roaming the universe in search of other adventures! But the silvery tinkle of Ora's laughter reached his ears. She was irresistible! He forgot his doubts as he hurried to his friend's cabin.

Mado was staring at the Europan maiden with a ludicrous expression of astonishment—gawping, Carr called it. And Ora was laughing at him.

"Your friend," she gurgled, "doesn't believe he's alive, or that I am, or you. Tell him we are."

Carr grinned. Mado did look funny at that. "Hello, old sock," he said, "had a bad dream?"

"Did I? Oh boy!" Mado rocked to and fro, his head in his hands. Then he displayed sudden intense interest. "Rapaju?" he asked. "His guards—the fleet—what's happened?"

"Ah ha! Now you know you're alive!" Carr laughed. "But the others are dead and gone. The fleet's gone to smash—and how!"

"But Carr. How did you do it? Tell me!"

Mado threw off his covers and clapped his friend on the back, a resounding thump that brought a gasp from Ora.

"Your Sargasso Sea did it. And it's a thing of the past, too. Wait till I tell you about it!"

Ora tripped from the room as Carr sat on the edge of the bunk to spin his yarn.

"But man alive!" Mado exclaimed when the story was finished. "Don't you know you've done a miraculous thing? I'd never have had the nerve. That damn creature out there had more than four times its former attracting energy. That's what made it impossible for the fleet to get away. And you—you lucky devil—you just doped it out right. The fleet of the Llotta gave you a tremendous push from astern when you used the repulsive energy. If they hadn't been there with their enormous mass to react against we'd all have been mincemeat now along with the Llotta. You Terrestrials sure can think fast! Me, now—Lord, if it had been me, I'd have thought of it after my spirit had departed to its reward—or punishment. Glory be! It's the greatest thing I ever heard of."

"Rats! You'd have done the same as I did. Probably would have missed it a mile instead of nearly getting caught as I did. A good thing the fleet's gone, though. Mars and Terra—Venus, too—they'll never know how close it was for them. Wouldn't have sense enough to appreciate it, anyway."

"They would if they ever got a taste of what the Llotta planned. But what's wrong with you Carr? You act sore. Want to go home?"

"Me? Don't be like that. No—I'd like to carry on as we planned. There's Saturn, Uranus and Neptune yet; Planet 9; a flock of satellites and asteroids. Oh, dammit!"

Mado looked his amazement. "Well, what's to prevent it?" he demanded. "The *Nomad's* still here, and so are we. I'm just as anxious to keep going as you are. Why not?"

But Carr did not reply. Why not, indeed? He strode from the cabin and into the control room. The *Nomad* was drifting in space, subject only to natural forces that swung it in a vast orbit around the sun. He started the generators and drove the vessel from her temporary orbit with rapid acceleration. Out—out into the jeweled blackness of the heavens. There was Jupiter out there, a bright orb that came suddenly very near when he centered it on the cross-hairs of the telescope.

The excited voices of Ora and Detis came to his ears. The booming speech of Mado. Why couldn't he be sensible and companionable as they were? But a perverse demon kept him at the controls. They'd think him a grouch. Well, maybe he was! But the vastness of the universe beckoned. New worlds to explore; mysteries to be solved; a life of countless new experiences! Anyone'd think he was the owner of the *Nomad*, the way he planned for the future.

They were in the control cabin now—Mado and Detis and Ora. A moment he hesitated, eyes glued to the telescope. Then, with a petulant gesture, he reached for the automatic control; locked it. Shouldn't be this way. They'd think him an awful cad. And they'd be right! He whirled to face them.

Detis was smiling. Mado gazed owlishly solemn. Ora clung to the arm of her father, and her long lashes hid the blue eyes that had played such havoc with the emotions of the Terrestrial.

"Carr," said Detis, gently, "we must thank you. You saved our lives, you know."

"Aw, forget it. Saved my own, too, didn't I? By a lucky break."

"It wasn't luck, Carr." Detis was gripping his hand now. "It was sheer grit and brains. You had them both. If you hadn't used them we'd all be corpses—or disintegrated—excepting Ora, perhaps. And you know the fate that awaited her. Instead, we are alive and well. The fleet is gone. Rapaju's body and that of his guard drift nameless in space where you disposed of them through the air-lock of the *Nomad.* The inner planets need fear no future invasion, for the resources of Ganymede have been expended in the one huge enterprise that has failed. All through your quick wit and bravery. No, it wasn't luck."

"Nonsense, Detis." Carr returned the pressure of the scientist's hand, smiling sheepishly. He pushed him away after a moment. He didn't want their gratitude or praise. Didn't know what he wanted. Ora still avoided meeting his gaze. "Nonsense," he repeated. "And now, please leave me. You, Detis. Mado, too. I'd like to be alone for a while—with Ora. Mind?"

Mado's owlish look broadened to a knowing grin as he backed into the passageway. Detis collided with the huge Martian in his eagerness to be out of the room. They were alone and Carr was on his feet. Nothing mattered now—excepting Ora. Suddenly she was in his arms, the fragrance of her hair in his nostrils.

Star gazing, the two of them. It was ridiculous! But the wonders of the universe held a new beauty now for Carr. The distant suns had taken on added brilliance. Still they beckoned.

"Carr," the girl whispered, after a time, "where are we going?"

"To Europa. Your home."

"To—to stay?"

"No." Carr was suddenly confident; determined. "We'll stop there to break the news. Then we'll be wedded, you and I, according to the custom of your people. Our honeymoon—years of it—will be spent in the *Nomad*, roving the universe. Mado'll agree, I know. Wanderers of the heavens we'll be, Ora. But we'll have each other; and when we've—you've—had enough of it, I'll be ready to settle down. Anywhere you say. Are you game?"

"Oh, Carr! How did you guess? It's just as we'd planned. Father and Mado and I. Didn't think I'd go, did you, you stupid old dear?"

"Why—why Ora." Carr was stammering now. He'd thought he was being masterful—making the plans himself. But she'd beat him to it, the adorable little minx! "I was a bit afraid," he admitted; "and I still can't believe that it's actually true. You're sure you want to?"

"Positive. Why Carr, I've always been a vagabond at heart. And now that I've found you we'll just be vagabonds together. Father and Mado will leave us very much to each other. Their scientific leanings, you know. And—oh—it'll just be wonderful!"

"It's you that'll make it wonderful, sweetheart."

Carr drew her close. The stars shone still more brightly and beckoned anew. Vagabonds, all of them! Like the gypsies of old, but with vastly more territory to roam. The humdrum routine of his old life seemed very far behind. He wondered what Courtney Davis would say if he could see him now. Wordless happiness had come to him, and he let his thoughts wander out into the limitless expanse of the heavens. Star gazing still—just he and Ora.

www.ingramcontent.com/pod-product-compliance
Ingram Content Group UK Ltd.
Pitfield, Milton Keynes, MK11 3LW, UK
UKHW040818280325
456847UK00003B/510

9 789367 247990